AF365565

THE LECTURES OF THE THREE DEGREES
IN CRAFT MASONRY

THE LECTURES
OF THE
THREE DEGREES
IN
CRAFT MASONRY

MASONICA

Publishers of the Ancient Craft

The Lectures Of The Three Degrees In Craf Masonry

(ANONYMOUS)

MASONICA®
Publishers of the Ancient Craft
www.freemasonrybooks.com

© 2020 ENTREACACIAS, S.L.

ENTREACACIAS, SL
[Publishing House]
Palacio Valdés, 3-5, 1ºC
33002 Oviedo - Asturias (Spain)
info@freemasonrybooks.com

First edition: November, 2020

ISBN: 978-84-18379-43-7
DL: AS 01276-2020

CONTENTS

The Lecture of the First Degree of Freemasonry   9
Introductory Address   11
Section One   13
Section Two   19
Section Three   31
Section Four   41
Section Five   49
Section Six   57
Section Seven   63

The Lecture of the Second Degree of Freemasonry   71
Introductory Address   73
Section One   75
Section Two   85
Section Three   93
Section Four   99
Section Five.   109

The Lecture of the Third Degree of Freemasonry   113
Introductory Address   115
Section One   117
Section Two   131
Section Three   137

THE LECTURE OF THE FIRST
DEGREE OF FREEMASONRY

TRACING BOARD—FIRST DEGREE.

INTRODUCTORY ADDRESS

Masonry, according to the general acceptation of the term, is an Art founded on the principles of Geometry, and directed to the service and convenience of mankind. But Freemasonry embracing a wider range, and having a more noble object in view, namely, the cultivation and improvement of the human mind, may, with more propriety, be called a Science, although its lessons for the most part are veiled in Allegory and illustrated by Symbols, inasmuch as, veiling itself under the terms of the former, it inculcates principles of the purest morality.

To draw aside this veil therefore, or, more properly speaking, to penetrate through its mysteries, is the object of our Masonic Lectures, and by a faithful and appropriate attention to them we hope ultimately to become acquainted with all its mysteries. The Lecture of this Degree is divided into seven Sections, and throughout the whole, virtue is depicted in its most beautiful colours, the duties of morality are everywhere strictly enforced.

The nature, character, the attributes and perfections of the Deity are faithfully delineated and forcibly portrayed, and are well calculated to influence our conduct towards Him, as our Father, Benefactor, and Moral Governor, as also in the proper discharge of the duties of social life.

SECTION ONE

The mode of Masonic instruction is the catechetical, or, in more familiar terms, by question and answer; therefore, from a previous conviction that you are a Mason, permit me to ask you in that character:

Q - As Free and Accepted Masons, how did you and I first meet?

A - On the Square.

Q - How do we hope to part?

A - On the Level.

Q - Why meet and part in that particular manner?

A - As Masons we should so act on the Square, as to enable us to part on the Level with all mankind, particularly a Brother.

Q - As a Mason whence come you?

A - The West.

Q - Whither directing your course?

A - The East.

Q - What inducement have you to leave the West, and go to the East?

A - To seek a Master, and from him to gain instruction.

Q - Who are you that want instruction?

A - A Free and Accepted Mason.

Q - What manner of man ought a Free and Accepted Mason to be?

A - A free man, born of a free woman, brother to a King, fellow to a Prince or to a beggar, if a Mason, and found worthy.

Q - Why freeborn?

A - In allusion to that grand festival which Abraham made at the weaning of his son Isaac, when Sarah, Abraham's wife, observing Ishmael, the son of Hagar the Egyptian bondwoman, teasing and perplexing her son, remonstrated with her husband, and said: Put away that bondwoman and her son, for such as he shall not inherit with the freeborn, even with my son Isaac. She spake as being endued with a prophetic spirit, well knowing that from Isaac's loins would spring a great and mighty people, who would serve the Lord with freedom, fervency, and zeal; and fearing that if the two youths were brought up together, Isaac might imbibe some of Ishmael's slavish principles; it being a general remark in those days, as well as the present, that the minds of slaves are more vitiated and less enlightened than those of the freeborn. This is the reason we, as Freemasons, give why every Mason ought to be freeborn; but in the present day, slavery being generally abolished, it has therefore been considered under our Constitution, that if a man be free, although he may not have been freeborn, he is eligible to be made a Mason.

Q - Why those equalities among Masons?

A - We are all created equal, which is strengthened by our Mason Oath.

Q - Generally speaking, as a Mason whence come you?

A - From a worthy and worshipful Lodge of Brothers and Fellows.

Q - What recommendation do you bring?

A - To greet your worship well.

Q - Any other recommendation?

A - Hearty good wishes.

Q - Since you bring nothing but hearty good wishes, what do you come here to do?

A - To learn to rule and subdue my passions, and make a further progress in Masonry.

Q - By this I presume you are a Mason?

A - I am so taken and accepted among Brothers and Fellows.

Q - How do you know yourself to be a Mason?

A - By the regularity of my initiation, repeated trials and approbations, and a willingness at all times to undergo an examination when properly called on.

Q - How do you demonstrate the proof of your being a Mason to others?

A - By Signs, Tokens, and the Perfect Points of my entrance.

Q - What are Signs?

A - All Squares, Levels, and Perpendiculars are true and proper signs to know a Mason by.

Q - What are Tokens?

A - Certain regular and friendly Grips, whereby we know a Brother in the dark as well as in the light.

Q - Will you give me the Points of your Entrance?

A - Give me the first, I will give you the second.

Q - What do you wish to Collect?

A - All Secrets and Mysteries of or belonging to Free and Accepted Masons in Masonry.

Q - This being open Lodge, you may safely reveal.

A - Of, At, and On.

Q - Of, At, and On what?

A - Of my own free will and accord; at the Door of the Lodge; on the Point of a Square presented to my naked left breast.

Q - When were you made a Mason?

A - When the sun was at its meridian.

Q - In this country Freemasons' Lodges are usually held in the evening: how do you account for that, which at first view appears a paradox?

A - The earth constantly revolving on its axis in its orbit round the sun, and Freemasonry being universally spread over its surface, it necessarily follows that the sun must always be at its meridian with respect to Freemasonry.

Q - What is Freemasonry?

A - A peculiar system of morality, veiled in allegory, and illustrated by symbols.

Q - Where were you made a Mason?

A - In the body of a Lodge, just, perfect, and regular.

Q - What is a Lodge of Freemasons?

A - An assemblage of Brethren, met to expatiate on the mysteries of the Craft.

Q - When met, what makes it just?

A - The Volume of the Sacred Law unfolded.

Q - What perfect?

A - Seven, or more, regularly made Masons.

Q - And what regular?

A - The charter or warrant of constitution.

Q - Why were you made a Mason?

A - For the sake of obtaining the Secrets of Masonry, and to be brought from darkness.

Q - Have Masons Secrets?

A - They have many invaluable ones.

Q - Where do they keep them?

A - In their Hearts.

Q - To whom do they reveal them?

A - None but Brothers and Freemasons.

Q - How do they reveal them?

A - By Signs, Tokens, and particular Words.

Q - As Masons, how do we hope to get at them?

A - By the help of a key.

Q - Does that key hang or lie?

A - It hangs.

Q - Why is the preference given to hanging?

A - It should always hang in a Brother's defense, and never lie to his prejudice.

Q - What does it hang by?

A - The thread of life, in the passage of utterance.

Q - Why is it so nearly connected with the heart?

A - Being an index of the mind, it should utter nothing but what the heart truly dictates.

Q - It is a curious key, of what metal is it composed?

A - No metal, it is the tongue of good report.

CHARGE

That excellent key, a Freemason's tongue, which should speak well of a Brother absent or present, but when unfortunately that cannot be done with honour and propriety, should adopt that excellent virtue of the Craft, which is Silence.

SECTION TWO

Q - Where were you first prepared to be made a Mason?

A - In my Heart.

Q - Where next?

A - In a convenient room adjoining the L.

Q - Who brought you to be made a Mason?

A - A friend, whom I afterwards found to be a Brother.

Q - Describe the mode of your preparation.

A - I was divested of metals and hoodwinked my right arm, left breast, and knee, were made bare, my right heel was slipshod, and a cable tow placed about my neck.

Q - Why were you divested of M.?

A - That I might bring nothing offensive or defensive into the Lodge to disturb its harmony.

Q - A second reason?

A - As I was received into Masonry in a state of poverty, it was to remind me to relieve indigent brethren, knowing them to be worthy, without detriment to myself or connections.

Q - A third reason?

A - At the building of King Solomon's Temple, there was not heard the sound of metallic tool.

Q - How could the building of so stately an edifice as King Solomon's Temple have been carried on and completed without the aid of metal tools?

A - The stones were hewn in the quarry, there squared, carved, marked, and numbered. The timber was felled and prepared in the forest of Lebanon, carved, marked, and numbered also; they were then floated to Joppa, thence conveyed on carriages to Jerusalem, and there set up with wooden mauls and implements prepared for that purpose.

Q - Why were the stones and timber prepared so far off?

A - To show the excellence of the Craft in those days, for although the materials were prepared at so great a distance, yet when they were brought to Jerusalem, and came to be put together, each piece fitted to that exact nicety, that it appeared more like the work of the Great Architect of the Universe than of human hands.

Q - Why were you hoodwinked?

A - That in case I had refused to go through any of the usual ceremonies required in making a Mason, I might have been led out of the Lodge without discovering its form.

Q - A second reason?

A - As I was received into Masonry in a state of darkness., it was to remind me to keep all the world so, with respect to our Masonic mysteries, unless they came legally by them as I was then about to do.

Q - A third reason?

A - That my heart might conceive before my eyes should discover.

Q - Why were you slipshod?

A - Our Lodges being considered to stand on Holy Ground, it al-
ludes to a certain passage of Scripture, where the Lord spoke
thus to Moses from the Burning Bush, "put off thy shoes
from off thy feet, for the place whereon thou standest is Holy
Ground."

Q - Being thus properly prepared, where were you conducted?

A - To the Door of the Lodge.

Q - How did you find that D.?

A - Shut and close Tyled.

Q - Whom was it Tyled by?

A - One whom I afterwards found to be the Tyler of the Lodge.

Q - His duty?

A - Being armed with a drawn Sword to keep off all intruders
and cowans to Masonry, and to see that the candidates are
properly prepared.

Q - Being in a state of darkness, how did you know it to be a
Door?

A - By meeting with an obstruction, and afterwards gaining admission.

Q - How did you gain admission?

A - By three distinct knocks.

Q - To what do these three distinct knocks allude?

A - An ancient and venerable exhortation Seek, and ye shall find;
ask, and ye shall have; knock, and it shall be opened unto
you.

Q - How did you apply that exhortation to your situation?

A - Having sought in my mind, I asked of my friend, he knocked, and the door of Freemasonry became open unto me.

Q - When the Masonic Door. became open unto you, who came to your assistance?

A - One whom I afterwards found to be the Inner Guard.

Q - What did he demand of your friend, or the Tyler?

A - Whom he had there.

Q - The Tyler's answer?

A - Mr. A. B., a poor candidate, in a state of darkness, who has been well and worthily recommended, regularly proposed and approved in open Lodge and now comes of his own free will and accord, properly prepared, humbly soliciting to be admitted to the mysteries. and privileges. of Freemasonry.

Q - What did the Inner Guard further demand?

A - How I hoped to obtain those privileges.

Q - Your answer?

A - By the help of God, being free, and of good report.

Q - How did the Inner Guard then proceed?

A - He desired me to halt, while he reported me to the Worshipful Master, who was afterwards pleased to order my admission.

Q - Were you admitted? And on what?

A - I was, on the Point of a sharp implement presented to my naked left breast.

Q - Why was the Point of a Sharp Implement presented to your naked left breast on your entrance into the Lodge?

A - To intimate to me that I was about to engage in something serious and solemn, likewise to distinguish the sex.

Q - When admitted into the Lodge, what was the first question put to you by the Master?

A - Mr. A. B., as no person can be made a Mason unless he is free and of mature age, I demand of you, are you a free man, and of the full age of twenty-one years? To which I answered in the affirmative.

Q - What were you then desired to do?

A - Kneel and receive the benefit of a Masonic prayer.

Q - Which I will thank you for.

A - Vouchsafe Thine aid, Almighty Father and Supreme Governor of the Universe, to our present convention, and grant that this Candidate for Freemasonry may so dedicate and devote his life to Thy service, as to become a true and 'faithful Brother amongst us. Endue him with a competency of Thy Divine wisdom, that, assisted by the secrets of our Masonic art he may the better be enabled to unfold the beauties of true godliness, to the honour and glory of Thy holy name.

So, mote it be.

Q.- After the recital of this prayer what was the next question put to you by Master?

A - In all cases of difficulty and danger in whom do you put your trust?

Q - Your answer?

A - In God.

Q - The Master's reply?

A - Right glad am I to find your faith well founded; relying on such sure support, you may safely rise, and follow your leader with a firm but humble confidence, for where the name of God is invoked we trust no danger can ensue.

Q - How did the Master then address the Lodge.

A - The brethren from the North, East, South, and West will take notice that Mr. A. B. is about to pass in view before them to show that he is the candidate, properly prepared, and fit and proper person to be made a Mason.

Q - How did your leader then dispose of you?

A - I being neither naked nor clothed barefoot nor shod, but in an humble, halting moving posture, he friendly took me by right hand, led me up the North, past the West to the East, down the South, and delivered me to the Senior. Warden in the West.

Q - What was required of you during your progress round the lodge?

A - To go through an examination by the Junior and Senior Wardens similar to that I had done at the door of the Lodge.

Q - Why were you led round in this spicuous manner?

A - It was figuratively to represent the seeming state of poverty and distress in which I was received into Masonry, on the miseries of which (if realised) were I for a moment to reflect, it could not fail to make that impression on my mind, as to cause me never to shut my cars unkindly to the cries of the distressed, particularly a Brother Mason, but listening with attention to their corn plaints, pity would flow from my breast, accompanied with that relief their necessities required and my ability could afford. It was likewise to show that I was the candidate properly prepared, and a fit and proper person to be made a Mason.

Q - Who are fit and proper persons to be made Masons?

A - Just, upright, and free men, of mature age, sound judgment, and strict morals.

Q - Why are the privileges of Masonry restricted to free men?

A - That the vicious habits of slavery might not contaminate the true principles of freedom on which the Order is founded.

Q - Why of mature age?

A - The better to be able to judge for ourselves, as well as the Fraternity at large.

Q - Why of sound judgment and strict morals?

A - That both by precept and example we may the better be enabled to enforce due obedience to those excellent laws and tenets laid down in Freemasonry.

Q - When delivered over to the Senior Warden the West, how did he proceed?

A - He presented me to the Worshipful Master, candidate properly prepared to be made Mason.

Q - The Master's answer?

A - Bro. Senior Warden, your presentation shall be attended to, for which purpose I shall ask a few questions to the candidate, which I trust he will answer with candour.

Q - The first of those questions?

A - Do you seriously declare on your honour, that, unbiased by the improper solicitation of friends against your own inclination, and uninfluenced by mercenary or other unworthy motive, you freely voluntarily offer yourself a candidate for the mysteries and privileges of Freemasonry?

Q - The second?

A - Do you likewise pledge yourself you are prompted to solicit those privileges by a favourable opinion preconceived of the Institution, a general desire of knowledge, and a sincere wish to render yourself more extensively serviceable to your fellow creatures?

Q - The third?

A - Do you further seriously declare your honour, that, avoiding fear on the one hand, and rashness on the other, you steadily persevere through the ceremony of your initiation, and if once admitted, will afterwards act and abide by the ancient usages and established customs of the Order?

To all of which, answers in the affirmative were given.

Q - What did the Master then order?

A - The Senior Warden to direct the Junior Deacon to instruct me to advance to the pedestal in due form.

Q - I will thank you to show the method of advancing from West to East in this degree.

A - (This is done.)

Q - Of what do those three irregular steps consist?

A - Right lines and angles.

Q - What do they morally teach?

A - Upright lives and well-squared actions.

Q - When placed before the Master in the East, how did he address you?

A - It is my duty to inform you that Masonry is free, and requires a perfect freedom of inclination in every Candidate for its mysteries; it is founded on the purest principles of piety and virtue; it possesses great and invaluable privileges; and in order to secure those privileges to worthy men, and we trust to worthy men alone, vows of fidelity are required; but let me assure you, that in those vows there is nothing incompatible with your civil, moral, or religious duties; are you therefore willing to take a solemn obligation, founded on the principles I have stated, to keep inviolate the secrets and mysteries of the Order? To which I gave my assent.

Q - Were you made a Mason?

A - I was, and that in due form.

Q - Describe the due form in which you were made a Mason.

A - I knelt on my left knee with my feet in the form of a square. With my right hand on the Volume of the Sacred Law, while my left was employed in supporting a pair of compasses presented to my naked left breast.

Q - Why were the Compasses presented to your naked left breast at the time of your initiation?

A - As the Compasses were then an emblem of torture to my body, so should the recollection ever prove to my mind, should I at any future period be about improperly to disclose any of those Masonic secrets I was then on the point of being entrusted with.

Q - In that attitude what were you about to do?

A - Take the Great and Solemn Obligation of a Mason.

Q - Which I will thank you for.

A - I, A. B., in the presence of the Great Architect of the Universe, and of this worthy worshipful, and warranted Lodge of Free and Accepted Masons, regularly assembled and properly dedicated, of my own free will and accord, do hereby and hereon sincerely and solemnly promise and swear, I will always hele, conceal, and never reveal any part or parts, point or points, of the secrets or mysteries of or belonging to Free and Accepted Masons in Masonry, which may heretofore have been known by me or shall now or at any future period be communicated to me, unless it be to a trusted and lawful Brother, or Brothers, and not even to him or them until after due trial, strict examination, or sure information from a well-known Brother that he or they are worthy of that confidence, or in the body of a just, perfect, and regular Lodge of ancient Freemasons. I further solemnly promise that I will not write those secrets, indite, carve, mark, engrave, or otherwise them delineate, or cause or suffer it to be done by others, if in my power to prevent it, on anything movable or immovable under the canopy of Heaven, whereby or whereon any letter, character, or figure, or the least trace of a letter, character, or figure, may become legible, or intelligible to myself or anyone in the world, so that our secret arts and hidden mysteries may improperly become known through my unworthiness. These several points I solemnly swear to observe, without evasion, equivocation, or mental reservation of any kind, under no less a penalty, on the violation of any of them, than that of having my throat cut across, my tongue torn from its root and my body buried in the rough sands of the sea whence the tide doth wash twice in the course of a natural day or the more effective punishment of being branded as a willfully perjured individual, void of all moral worth, and totally unfit to be received into this worshipful Lodge, or any other warranted Lodge, or society of men who prize honour and. virtue above the external advantages of rank and fortune. So help me God, and keep me steadfast in this my Great and Solemn Obligation of an Entered Apprentice Freemason.

Q - Having taken the Solemn Obligation of a Mason, how did the Master address you?

A - What you have repeated may be considered but a serious promise; as a pledge of your fidelity, and to render it a Solemn Obligation you will seal it with your lips on the Volume of the Sacred Law.

Q - How did he further address you?

A - Having been kept for a considerable time in a state of darkness, what in your present situation is the predominant wish of your heart.

Q - Your answer?

A - Light. To which the Junior Deacon., by the Worshipful Master's command, was pleased to restore me.

Q - Having been restored to the blessing of material Light, what were then pointed out to your attention?

A - The three great though emblematic light in Freemasonry, which are, the Volume of the Sacred Law, the Square and Compasses.

Q - Their uses?

A - The Sacred Words are to govern our faith; the Square to regulate our actions; and the Compasses. to keep us in due bounds with all mankind, particularly our Brethren in Freemasonry.

Q - How did the Master then proceed?

A - He friendly took me by the right hand, and said, Rise, newly Obligated Brother among Masons.

CHARGE

The heart that conceals, and the Tongue that never improperly reveals, any or either of the secrets or mysteries of or belonging to Free and Accepted Masons in Masonry.

SECTION THREE

Q - After you were raised from your kneeling posture, what were you enabled to discover?

A - The three lesser lights.

Q - How are they situated?

A - East, South, and West.

Q - For what purpose?

A - To show the due course of the Sun, which rises in the East, gains its meridian lustre in the South, and sets in the West; likewise to light men to, at, and from labour.

Q - Why is there none in the North?

A - The Sun being then below our horizon, darts no ray of light from that quarter to this our hemisphere.

Q - What do those three lesser lights represent?

A - The Sun, Moon, and Master of the Lodge.

Q - Why the Sun, Moon, and Master?

A - The Sun to rule the day, the Moon to govern the night, and the Master to rule and direct his Lodge.

Q - Why is the Master of a Freemason's Lodge compared to those grand luminaries?

A - As it is by the benign influence of the Sun and Moon that we, as men, are enabled to perform the duties of social life, so it is by the kind care and instruction of the Worshipful. Master, that we, as Masons, are enabled to perform those duties the Craft require of us.

Q - After the lesser lights were explained how did the Master address you?

A - Brother A. B., by your meek and candid behaviour this evening, you have escaped two great dangers, but there is a third which will await you until the latest period of your existence. The dangers you have escaped are those of death stabbing and death strangulation for on your entrance into the Lodge this Dagger. was presented to your naked left breast, so that had you rashly attempted to rush forward, you would have been accessory to your own death. by stabbing whilst the Brother who held it would have remained firm, and done his duty. There was likewise this Cabletow with a running noose about your neck which would have rendered any attempt at retreat equally fatal; but the danger which will await you until your latest hour is the penalty of your obligation, having your throat cut across, your tongue torn from its roots and your body buried in the rough sands of the sea whence the tide doth wash twice in the course of a natural day, should you improperly disclose the Secrets of Masonry.

Q - How did he further address you?

A - Having taken the Great and Solemn Obligation of a Mason, I am now permitted to inform you that there are several Degrees in Freemasonry, and peculiar secrets restricted to each. These, however, are not communicated indiscriminately, but are conferred on candidates according to merit and abilities. I shall therefore, proceed to intrust you with the secrets of this Degree, or those marks by which we are known to each other, and distinguished from the rest of the world; but must premise for your general information, that all Squares, Levels and Perpendiculars are true and proper signs to know a Mason by; you are therefore expected to stand perfectly erect, your feet formed in a Square; your body being thus considered an emblem of your mind, and your feet of the rectitude of your actions.

Q - What did the Master, then direct you to do?

A - Take a step towards him with my left foot, bringing the right heel into its hollow; that, he informed me, is the first regular step in Freemasonry and it is in this position that the signs of the degree are communicated.

Q - Of what do those signs consist?

A - A Sign, Token, and Word.

Q - I will thank you for the Sign in due form.

A - (Which is given.)

Q - Communicate the Token to.

A - (Which is done.)

Q - Is that correct?

A - It is, Worshipful Master.

Q - What does that demand?

A - A Word.

Q - Give me that Word.

A - At my initiation I was taught to be cautious; but with you as a brother I will letter or halve it with you.

Q - Which you please, and begin.

A - (It is then given).

Q - Whence is this Word derived?

A - From the left hand pillar at the Porchway or Entrance. of King Solomon's Temple, so named after the Great Grandfather of David and a Prince and Ruler in Israel.

Q - The import of the Word?

A - In Strength.

Q - Having been Obligated and intrusted, were you invested?

A - I was, with the distinguishing badge of a Mason, which the Senior Warden informed me is more ancient than the Golden Fleece, or Roman Eagle, more honourable than the Garter, or any other Order in existence, being the badge of innocence, and the bond of friendship: he strongly exhorted me ever to wear and consider it as such; and further informed me, that if I never disgraced that badge, it would never disgrace me.

Q - Repeat the address you then received from the Master.

A - Let me add to the observations of the Senior Warden, that you are never to put on that badge should you be about to visit a Lodge in which there is a Brother with whom you are at variance, or against whom you entertain animosity; in such cases, it is expected that will invite him to withdraw, in order amicably to settle your differences, which being happily effected, you may then clothe yourselves, enter the Lodge, and work with that love and harmony which should at all times characterise Freemasons. But if, unfortunately, your differences be of such a nature as not to be so easily adjusted, it were better one or both of you retire, than that the that harmony of the Lodge should be disturbed by your presence.

Q - Where were you then ordered to be placed?

A - At the North East part of the Lodge.

Q - Repeat the charge.

A - It is customary at the erection of all stately and superb edifices to lay the first or foundation stone at the North. East cor-
ner of the building; you, being newly admitted into Masonry,
are placed at the North East part of the Lodge, figuratively to
represent that stone: and from the foundation laid this evening may you raise a superstructure perfect in its parts and
honourable to the builder. You now stand to all external appearance a just and upright Mason, and I give it you in strong
terms of recommendation ever to continue and act as such;
indeed, I shall immediately proceed to put your principles in
some measure to the test, by calling upon you to exercise that
virtue which may justly be denominated the distinguishing
characteristic of a Freemason's heart I mean Charity. I need
not here dilate on its excellencies; no doubt it has often been
felt and practiced by you; suffice it to say, it has the approbation of heaven and earth, and, like its sister Mercy, blesses
him who gives as well as him who receives. In a society so
widely extended as Freemasonry, the branches of which are
spread over the four quarters of the globe, it cannot be de-
nied that we have many members of rank and opulence, neither can it be concealed that among the thousands who range
under its banners, there are some who, perhaps from circumstances of unavoidable calamity and misfortune, are reduced
to the lowest ebb of poverty and distress. On their behalf it is
our usual custom to awaken the feelings of every newmade

Brother, by such a claim on his charity as his circumstances in life may fairly warrant; whatever, therefore, you feel disposed to give, you will deposit with the Junior Deacon; it will be thankfully received, and faithfully applied.

Q - Your answer?

A - That I had been divested of everything valuable previously to entering the Lodge, or I would give freely.

Q - The Master's reply?

A - I congratulate you on the honourable sentiments by which you are actuated, likewise on the inability which in the present instance precludes you from gratifying them; believe me, this trial was not made with a view to sport with your feelings; far be from us any such intention; it was done for three especial reasons.

Q - The first of those reasons?

A - To put my principles to the test.

Q - The second?

A - To evince to the Brethren that I had neither metal nor metallic substance about me, for if I had, the ceremony of my initiation, thus far must have been repeated.

Q - The third?

A - As a warning to my own heart, that should I at any future period meet a brother in distressed circumstances who might solicit my assistance, I would remember the peculiar moment I was received into Masonry, poor and penniless and cheerfully embrace the opportunity of practicing that virtue I had professed to admire.

Q - What did the Master then present to you?

A - The working tools of an Entered Apprentice Freemason which are the 24-inch Gauge, the common Gavel and Chisel.

Q - Their uses?

A - The 24-inch Gauge is to measure our work, the common Gavel to knock off all superfluous knobs and excrescences, and the Chisel to further smooth and prepare the stone, and render it fit for the hands of the more expert workman.

Q - But as we are not all operative Masons, but rather Free and Accepted, or speculative, how do we apply these tools to our morals?

A - In this sense, the 24-inch Gauge represents the 24 hours of the day, part to be spent in prayer to Almighty God, part in labour and refreshment, and part in serving a Friend or Brother in time of need, without detriment to ourselves or connections. The common Gavel represents the force of conscience, which should keep down all vain and unbecoming thoughts which might obtrude during any of the aforementioned periods, so that our words and actions may ascend unpolluted to the throne of grace. The Chisel points out to us the advantages of education, by which means alone we are rendered fit members of regularly organised society.

Q - How did the Master then address you?

A - As in the course of the evening you will be called on for certain fees for your initiation, it is proper you should know by what authority we act. This is our charter or warrant from the Grand Lodge of England, which is for your inspection on this or any future evening. This is the book of Constitutions, and

these are our byelaws, both of which I recommend to your serious perusal, as by one you will be instructed in the duties
you owe to the craft in general, and by the other, in those you
owe to this Lodge in particular.

Q - What permission did you then receive?

A - To retire, in order to restore myself to my personal comforts,
and the Worshipful Master informed me that on my return
to the Lodge he would call my attention to a charge, founded
on the excellences of the Institution and the qualifications of
its members.

Q - When placed at the North East part of the Lodge, assisted by
the three lesser lights, what were you enabled to discover?

A - The form of the Lodge.

Q - What form?

A - A parallelopipedon.

Q - Describe its dimensions.

A - In length from East to West, in breadth between North and
South, in depth from the surface of the earth to the centre,
and even as high as the Heavens.

Q - Why is a Freemason's Lodge described of this vast extent?

A - To show the universality of the science; likewise, that a Mason's charity should know no bounds save those of prudence.

CHARGE

All poor and distressed Masons, wherever dispersed over the face of earth, and Water, wishing them a speedy relief from their sufferings, and a safe return to their native country, if they desire it.

SECTION FOUR

Q - On what ground do our Lodges stand?

A - Holy Ground.

Q - Why on Holy Ground?

A - Because the first Lodge was consecrated.

Q - Why was it consecrated?

A - On account of three grand offerings thereon made, which met with Divine approbation.

Q - Which I will thank you to specify.

A - First, the ready compliance of Abraham with the will of God in not refusing to offer up his son Isaac as a burnt sacrifice, when it pleased the Almighty to substitute a more agreeable victim in his stead. Secondly, the many pious prayers and ejaculations of King David, which actually appeased the wrath of God, and stayed a pestilence which then raged among his people, owing to his inadvertently having had them numbered. And thirdly, the many thanksgivings, oblations. burnt sacrifices, and costly offerings which Solomon, King of Israel, made at the completion, dedication, and consecration of the Temple at Jerusalem to God's service. Those three did then, do now, and I trust ever will render the ground of Freemasonry holy.

Q - How are our Lodges situated?

A - Due East and West.

Q - Why?

A - Because all places of Divine worship as well as Masons' regular, well-formed, constituted Lodges, are or ought to be so situated.

Q - For which we assign three Masonic reasons; I will thank you for the first.

A - The Sun, the Glory of the Lord, rises, in the East and sets in the West.

Q - The second?

A - Learning originated in the East, and thence spread its benign influence to the West.

Q - The third, last, and grand reason?

A - Whenever we contemplate on the works of the creation, how ready and cheerful ought we to be to adore the Almighty Creator, who has never left Himself without a living witness among men. From the earliest period of time, we have been taught to believe in the existence of a Deity. We read of Abel bringing a more acceptable offering to the Lord than his brother Cain; of Enoch walking with God; of Noah, being a just and upright man in his day and generation, and a teacher of righteousness; of Jacob wrestling with an angel, prevailing, and thereby obtaining a blessing for himself and posterity. But we never hear or read of any place being set apart for the public solemnisation of Divine worship, until after the happy deliverance of the children of Israel from their Egyptian bondage, which it pleased the Almighty to effect with a high hand and an outstretched arm, under the conduct of His faithful servant Moses, according to a promise made their forefather, Abraham, that He would make of his seed a great and mighty people, even as the stars in Heaven for number, and the sand of the sea for multitude. And as they were about to possess the gate of their enemies, and inherit the promised land, the Almighty thought proper to reveal to them those three most excellent institutions-viz., the Moral, Ceremonial, and judicial Laws. And for the better solemnisation of Divine worship, as well as a receptacle for the Books and Tables of the Law, Moses caused a Tent or Tabernacle to be erected in the wilderness, which by God's especial command was situated due East and West, for Moses did everything according to a pattern shown him by the Lord on Mount Sinai. This Tent or Tabernacle proved afterwards to be the ground-plan, in respect to situation, of that most magnificent Temple built at Jerusalem by that wise and mighty Prince, King Solomon, whose regal splendour and unparalleled lustre far transcend our ideas. This is the third, last, and grand reason. I as a Freemason give, why all. places of Divine worship, as well as Masons' regular, well-formed, constituted Lodges are or ought to be so situated.

Q - What supports a Freemason's Lodge?

A - Three great Pillars.

Q - What are they called?

A - Wisdom, Strength, and Beauty.

Q - Why Wisdom, Strength, and Beauty?

A - Wisdom to contrive, Strength to support, and Beauty to adorn.

Q - Moralise them.

A - Wisdom to conduct us in all our undertakings, Strength to support us under all our difficulties, and Beauty to adorn the inward man.

Q - Illustrate them.

A -The Universe is the Temple of the Deity whom we serve; Wisdom, Strength and Beauty are about His throne as pillars of His works, for His Wisdom is infinite His Strength omnipotent, and Beauty shines through the whole of the creation in symmetry and order. The Heavens He has stretched forth as a canopy; the earth He has planted as a footstool; He crowns His Temple with Stars as with a diadem, and with his hand He extends the power and glory. The Sun and Moon are messengers of His will, and all His law is concord. The three great pillars supporting a Freemason's Lodge are emblematic of those Divine attributes, and further represent Solomon King of Israel, Hiram, King of Tyre and Hiram Abif.

Q - Why those three great personages?

A - Solomon King of Israel for his wisdom in building, completing, and dedicating the Temple at Jerusalem to God's service; Hiram King. of Tyre for his strength in supporting him with men and materials; and Hiram Abif. for his curious and masterly workmanship in beautifying and adorning the same.

Q - As we have no noble Order of Architecture known by the names of Wisdom, Strength, and Beauty, to which do they refer?

A - The three most celebrated, which are the Ionic, Doric, and Corinthian.

Q - Name the covering of a Freemason's Lodge.

A - A Celestial Canopy of divers colours, even the Heavens.

Q - As Masons, how can we hope to arrive there?

A - By the assistance of a Ladder, in Scripture called Jacob's Ladder.

Q - Why was it called Jacob's ladder?

A - Rebecca, the beloved wife of Isaac, knowing by Divine inspiration that a peculiar blessing was vested in the soul of her husband, was desirous to obtain it for her favourite son Jacob, though by birthright belonged to Esau her first-born. Jacob had no sooner fraudulently obtained his father's blessing, than he was obliged to flee from the wrath of his brother, who in a moment of rage and disappointment had threatened to kill him. Arid as he journeyed towards Padanaram, in the land of Mesopotamia (where by his parents' strict command he was enjoined to go), being weary and benighted on a desert plain, he lay down to rest, taking the Earth for his bed, a stone for his pillow, and the Canopy of Heaven for a covering. He there in a vision saw a Ladder, the top of which reached to the Heavens, and the Angels of the Lord ascending and descending thereon. It was then the Almighty entered into a solemn covenant with Jacob, that if he would abide by His laws, and keep His commandments, He would not only bring him again to his father's house in peace and prosperity, but would make of his seed a great and mighty people.

This was amply verified, for after a lapse of twenty years Jacob returned to his native country, was kindly received by his brother Esau, his favourite son Joseph was afterwards, by Pharaoh's appointment, made second man in Egypt, and the children of Israel, highly favoured by the Lord, became, in process of time, one of the greatest and most mighty Nations on the face of the earth,

Q - Of how many staves or rounds was this Ladder composed?

A - Of many staves or rounds, which point out as many moral virtues, but three principal ones, which are, FAITH, HOPE, and CHARITY.

Q - Why Faith, Hope, and Charity?

A - Faith in the Great Architect of the Universe; Hope in Salvation; and to be in Charity with all men.

Q - I will thank you to define FAITH.

A - Is the foundation of justice, the bond of amity, and the chief support of civil society. We live and walk by Faith. By it we have a continual acknowledgment of a Supreme Being. By Faith we have access to the Throne of grace, are justified, accepted, and finally received. A true and sincere Faith is the evidence of things not seen, but the substance of those hoped for. This well maintained and answered in our Masonic profession, will bring us to those blessed mansions, where we shall be eternally happy with God the Great Architect of the Universe.

Q - HOPE?

A - Is an anchor of the soul, both sure and steadfast, and enters into that within the veil. Then let a firm reliance on the Almighty's faithfulness animate our endeavours, and teach us to fix our desires within the limits of His most blessed promises. So shall success attend us. If we believe a thing impossible, our despondency may render it so, but he who perseveres in a just cause will ultimately overcome all difficulties.

Q - CHARITY?

A - Lovely in itself, is the brightest ornament which can adorn our Masonic profession. It is the best test and surest proof of the sincerity of our religion. Benevolence, rendered by Heaven- born Charity, is an honour to the nation whence it springs, is nourished, and cherished. Happy is the man who has, sown in his breast, the seeds of benevolence; he envies not his neighbour, he believes not a tale reported to his prejudice, he forgives the injuries of men, and endeavours to blot them from his recollection. Then, Brethren., let us remember, that we are Free and Accepted Masons; ever ready to listen to him who craves our assistance; and from him who is in want, let us not withhold a liberal hand. So shall a heartfelt satisfaction reward our labours, and the produce of love and Charity will most assuredly follow.

Q - On what does this Ladder rest in a Freemason's Lodge?

A - The Volume of the Sacred Law.

Q - Why does it rest there?

A - Because by the doctrines contained in that Holy Book, we are taught to believe in the dispensations of Divine Providence; which belief strengthens our Faith, and enables us to ascend the first step. This Faith naturally creates in us a Hope of becoming partakers of the blessed promises therein recorded; which Hope enables us to ascend the second step. But the third and last, being Charity, comprehends the whole; and the Mason who is possessed of this virtue in its most ample sense, may justly be deemed to have attained the summit of his profession; figuratively speaking, an ethereal mansion, veiled from mortal eyes by the starry firmament, emblematically depicted in our Lodges by seven Stars, which have an allusion to as many regularly made Masons; without which number no Lodge is perfect, neither can any candidate be legally initiated into the Order.

CHARGE

May every Mason attain the summit of his profession, where the just will most assuredly meet their due reward.

SECTION FIVE

Q - Of what is the interior of a Freemason's Lodge composed?

A - Ornaments, Furniture, and jewels.

Q - Name the Ornaments.

A - The Mosaic Pavement, the Blazing Star, and the Indented or Tessellated Border.

Q - Their situations?

A -The Mosaic Pavement is the beautiful flooring of the Lodge; the Blazing Star the glory in the centre; and the Indented or Tessellated Border the skirtwork round the same.

Q - I will thank you to moralise them.

A - The Mosaic Pavement may justly be deemed the beautiful flooring of a Freemason's Lodge, by reason of its being variegated and chequered. This points out the diversity of objects which decorate and adorn the creation, the animate as well as the inanimate parts thereof. The Blazing Star, or glory in the centre, refers us to the Sun, which enlightens the earth, and by its benign influence dispenses its blessings to mankind in general. The Indented or Tessellated Border refers us to the Planets, which, in their various revolutions form a beautiful border or skirtwork round that grand luminary, the Sun, as the other does round that of a Freemason's Lodge.

Q - Why was Mosaic work introduced into Freemasonry?

A - As the steps of man are trod in the various and uncertain incidents of life, and his days are variegated and chequered by a strange contrariety of events, his passage through this existence, though sometime attended by prosperous circumstances, is often beset by a multitude of evils; hence is our Lodge. furnished with Mosaic work, to point out the uncertainty of all things here on earth. Today we may travel in prosperity tomorrow we may totter on the uneven path of weakness, temptation, and adversity. Then while such emblems are before us, we are morally instructed not to boast of anything but to give heed to our ways, to walk up rightly and with humility before God, there being no station in life on which pride can with stability be founded; for though some are born to more elevated situations than others, yet, when in the grave, we are all on the level, death destroying all distinctions; and while our feet tread on this Mosaic work, let our ideas recur to the original whence we copy; let us, as good men and Masons, act as the dictates of reason prompt us, to practice charity, maintain harmony, and endeavour to live in unity and brotherly love.

Q - Name the furniture of the Lodge.

A - The Volume of the Sacred Law, the Compasses, and Square.

Q - Their uses?

A - The Sacred Words. are to rule and govern our faith, on them we Obligate. our candidates for Freemasonry. So are the Compasses. and Square, when united, to regulate our lives and actions.

Q - From whom is the first derived, and to whom do the other two more properly belong?

A - The Sacred Volume is derived from God to man in general; the Compasses belong to the Grand Master in particular; and the Square to the whole Craft.

Q - Why the Sacred Volume from God to man in general?

A - Because the Almighty has been pleased to reveal more of His Divine will in that Holy Book than He has by any other means.

Q - Why the Compasses to the Grand Master in particular?

A - That, being the chief instrument made use of in the formation of Architectural plans and designs, is peculiarly appropriated to the Grand Master, as an emblem of his dignity; he being the Chief, Head, and Governor of the Craft.

Q - And why the Square to the whole Craft?

A - The Craft being Obligated within the Square are consequently bound to act thereon.

Q - Before our ancient brethren had the benefit of such regular, well-formed, constituted Lodges as we now enjoy, where did they assemble?

A - On high hills and in low vales, even in the valley of Jehoshaphat, and many other secret places.

Q - Why so high, low, and very secret?

A - The better to observe all who might ascend or descend; that if a stranger should approach, the Tyler might give timely notice to the Master to hail the brethren, close the Lodge, put by the jewels, and thereby prevent any of our Masonic secrets from being illegally obtained.

Q - You speak of jewels, and seem careful of them; how many are
there in the Lodge?

A - Three movable, and three immovable.

Q - Name the movable jewels?

A - The Square, Level, and Plumb Rule.

Q - Their uses?

A - The Square is to try, and adjust rectangular corners of buildings, and assist in bringing rude matter into due form; the
Level to lay levels, and prove horizontals; the Plumb Rule to
try, and adjust uprights, while fixing them on their proper bases.

Q - It would appear from this that they are mere mechanical
tools; why do you call them jewels?

A - On account of their moral tendency, which renders them
jewels of inestimable value.

Q - I will thank you to moralise them.

A - The Square teaches us to regulate our lives and actions according to the Masonic line and rule, and to harmonise our
conduct in this life, so as to render us acceptable to that Divine Being from whom all goodness springs, and to whom we
must give an account of all our actions.

The Level demonstrates that we are all sprung from the same
stock, partakers of the same nature, and sharers in the same
hope; and although distinctions among men are necessary to
preserve subordination, yet ought no eminence of situation
make us forget that we are Brothers; for he who is placed on
the lowest spoke of fortune's wheel is equally entitled to our

regard; as a time will come and the wisest of us knows not how soon when all distinctions, save those of goodness and virtue, shall cease, and Death, the grand leveller of all human greatness, reduce us to the same state.

The infallible Plumb Rule., which, like Jacob's ladder, connects Heaven and Earth, is the criterion of rectitude and truth. It teaches us to walk justly and uprightly before God and man; neither turning to the right nor left from the paths of virtue. Not to be an enthusiast, persecutor, or slanderer of religion; neither bending towards avarice, injustice, malice, revenge, nor the envy and contempt of mankind, but giving up every selfish propensity which might injure others. To steer the bark of this life over the seas of passion, without quitting the helm of rectitude, is the highest perfection to which human nature can attain., and as the builder raises his column by the level and perpendicular, so ought every Mason to conduct himself towards this world; to observe a due medium between avarice and profusion; to hold the scales of justice with equal poise; to make his passions and prejudices coincide with the just line of his conduct; and in all his pursuits to have Eternity in view. Thus the Square teaches morality, the Level equality, and the Plumb Rule justness and uprightness of life and actions.

Q - Why are they called movable jewels?

A - Because they are worn by the Master and his Wardens, and are transferable to their successors on nights of Installation.

Q - What is the Master distinguished by?

A - The Square; and why, Worshipful. Master?

W. M. - As it is by the assistance of the Square that rude matter is brought into due form, so it is by the Square. conduct of the Master that animosities are made to subside should any unfortunately arise among the Brethren, that the business of Masonry may be conducted with harmony and decorum.

Q - Brother Senior Warden, why are you distinguished by the Level?

S.W. - That being an emblem of equality, points out the equal measures I am bound to pursue in conjunction with your Worship Master in the well ruling and governing of the Lodge.

Q - Brother Junior Warden, why are you distinguished by the Plumb Rule?

J.W. - That being an emblem of uprightness, points out the integrity of the measures I am bound to pursue, in conjunction with your Worshipful Master and my Brother Senior Warden, in the well ruling and governing of the Lodge, particularly in the examination of visitors, lest through my neglect any unqualified person should gain admission to our assemblies, and the Brethren be thereby innocently led to violate their Obligations.

Q - Name the Immovable jewels?

A - The Tracing Board, the Rough and Perfect Ashlars.

Q - Their uses?

A - The Tracing Board is for the Master to lay lines and draw designs on; the Rough Ashlar for the Entered Apprentice to work, mark, and indent on; and the Perfect Ashlar for the experienced craftsman to try and adjust his jewels on.

Q - Why are these called Immovable jewels?

A - Because they lie open and Immovable in the Lodge for the Brethren to moralise on.

Q - There is a beautiful comparison between the immovable jewels and the furniture of the Lodge, which I will thank you for.

A - As the Tracing Board is for the Master to lay lines and draw designs on, the better to enable the Brethren to carry on the intended structure with regularity and propriety, so the Volume of the Sacred Law may justly be deemed the spiritual Tracing Board of the great Architect of the Universe, in which are laid down such Divine laws and moral plans, that were we conversant therein, and adherent thereto, would bring us to an ethereal mansion not made with hands, eternal in the Heavens. The Rough Ashlar is a stone, rough and unhewn as taken from the quarry, until, by the industry and ingenuity of the workman, it is modeled, wrought into due form, and rendered fit for the intended structure. This represents man in his infant or primitive state rough and unpolished as that stone, until by the kind care and attention of his parent or guardians, in giving him a liberal and virtuous education, his mind becomes cultivated, and he is thereby rendered a fit member of civilised society. The Perfect Ashlar is a stone of a true die or square, fit only to be tried by the Square and Compasses. This represents man in the decline of years, after a regular well-spent life in acts of piety and virtue, which can no otherwise be tried and approved than by the Square of

God's Word, and the Compass of his own self-convincing conscience.

Q - The Lodge being finished, furnished, and decorated, to whom do we dedicate it as a general Law?

A - God and His service.

Q - To whom next?

A - King Solomon.

Q - Why to King Solomon?

A - He being the first Prince who excelled in Masonry, and under whose royal patronage many of our Masonic mysteries obtained their first sanction.

CHARGE

The past Grand Patrons of Masonry.

SECTION SIX

Q - Name the first point in Freemasonry.

A - Left knee bare and bent.

Q - Why is that called the first point?

A - On my bended knees I was taught to adore my Creator, on my left knee bare and bent I was initiated into Masonry.

Q - There is a chief point?

A - To be happy ourselves, and to communicate happiness to others.

Q - A principal point?

A - A point within a circle.

Q - Define that point.

A - In all regular, well-formed, constituted Lodges, there is a point within a circle round which the Brethren cannot err. This circle is bounded between North. and South by two grand parallel lines, one representing Moses and the other King Solomon. On the upper part of this circle rests the Volume of the Sacred Law, supporting Jacob's ladder, the top of which reaches to the heavens; and were we as conversant in that Holy Book, and as adherent to the doctrines therein contained, as those parallels were, it would bring us to Him who would not deceive us, neither will He suffer deception. In going round this circle, we must necessarily touch on both those parallel lines likewise on the Sacred Volume, and whilst a Mason keeps himself thus circumscribed, he cannot err.

Q - Name the grand principles on which the Order is founded.

A - Brotherly Love, Relief, and Truth.

Q - I will thank you to define BROTHERLY LOVE.

A - By the exercise of Brotherly Love, we are taught to regard the whole human species as one family, the high and low, the rich and poor, created by One Almighty Being, and sent into the world for the aid, support, a protection of each other. On this principle Masonry unites men of every country, sect and opinion, and by its dictates conciliate true friendship among those who might otherwise have remained at a perpetual distance.

Q - RELIEF?

A - To relieve the distressed is a duty incumbent on all men, particularly Masons who are linked together in one indissoluble chain of sincere affection; hence, to soothe the unhappy, sympathize in their misfortunes compassionate their miseries, and restore peace to their troubled minds, is the grand aim we have in view; on this basis we establish our friendships and form our connections.

Q - TRUTH?

A - Is a Divine attribute and the foundation of every Masonic virtue; to be good men and true is a lesson we are taught at our Initiation; on this grand theme we contemplate, and by its unerring dictates, endeavour to regulate our lives and actions. Hence, hypocrisy and deceit are, or ought to be, unknown to us, sincerity and plain dealing are our distinguishing characteristics, whilst the heart and tongue join in promoting each other's welfare, and rejoicing in the prosperity of the Craft.

Q - How many original forms have we in Freemasonry?

A - Four.

Q - I will thank you to show Masonically to which parts of the body they refer.

A -The throat, refers to the penalty contained in my Obligation, implying that as a man of honour and a Mason I would rather have my throat cut across, my tongue torn from its roots and my body buried in the rough sands of the sea whence the tide doth wash twice in the course of a natural day rather than betray any of the secret or secrets, mystery or mysteries of Masonry. Next the breast, where those secrets are deposited safe and secure from the popular world who are not Masons. The hand placed on the Volume of the Sacred Law, as a token of my assent to the Obligation of a Mason. The fist formed in a square at the North East part of the Lodge denoting a just and upright Mason.

Q - They have a further allusion.

A - To the four cardinal virtues, namely: Temperance, Fortitude, Prudence, and Justice.

Q - I will thank you to define TEMPERANCE.

A - Is that due restraint of the passion and affections, which renders the body tame and governable, and relieves the mind from the allurements of vice. This virtue ought to be the constant practice of every Mason as he is thereby taught to avoid excess, or the contracting of any vicious or licentious habits, whereby he might, unwarily, be led to betray his trust, and subject himself the penalty contained in his Obligation.

Q - FORTITUDE?

A - Is that noble and steady purport of the soul, which is equally distant from rashness and cowardice; it enables us to undergo any pain labour, danger, or difficulty, when thought necessary, or deemed prudentially expedient. This virtue, like the former ought to be deeply impressed on the breast of every Mason, as a fence and security against any attempts which might be made either by threats or violence, to extort from him any of those Masonic secrets he has so solemnly engaged himself to HELE, conceal, and never improperly reveal; the illegal revealing of which might prove a torment to his mind, as the Compasses were emblematically to his body when extended to his naked left breast at time of his Initiation.

Q - PRUDENCE?

A - Teaches us to regulate our lives and actions according to the dictates of reason, and is that habit of mind whereby men wisely judge, and prudentially determine, all things relative to their temporal and eternal happiness. This virtue ought to be the distinguishing characteristic of every Free and Accepted Mason, not only for the good regulation of his own life and actions, but as a pious example to the popular world who are not Masons, and ought to be nicely attended to in strange or mixed companies, never to let drop or slip the least Sign, Token, or Word, whereby any of our Masonic secrets might be illegally obtained; ever having in recollection that period of time when he was placed before the Worshipful Master in the East with his left knee made bare and his bent right foot formed in a square while his right hand was placed on the Volume of the Sacred Law.

Q - JUSTICE?

A - Is that station or boundary of right, by which we are taught to render to every man his just due, and that without distinction. This virtue is not only consistent with the Divine and human Law, but is the standard and cement of civil society. Without the exercise of this Virtue, universal confusion would ensure, lawless force would overcome the principles of equity, and social intercourse no longer exist; and as justice in a great measure constitutes the really good man, so it ought to be the invariable practice of every Free and Accepted Mason never to deviate from the minutest principles thereof, ever having in mind the time he was placed at the North East part of the Lodge, feet formed in a square being evident, when he received that excellent injunction from the Worshipful Master to be just and upright in all things; alluding to the Perpendicular.

CHARGE

May Brotherly Love, Relief, and Truth, in conjunction with Temperance, Fortitude, Prudence, and Justice, distinguish Free and Accepted Masons till time shall be no more.

SECTION SEVEN

Q - How many sorts of Masons are there?

A - Two: Free and Accepted, and Operative.

Q - Which of those are you?

A - Free and Accepted.

Q - What do you learn by being a Free and Accepted Mason?

A - Secrecy, Morality, and Good Fellowship.

Q - What do Operative Masons learn?

A - The useful rules of Architecture; to hew, square, and mould stones into the formation required for the purposes of building; and unite them by means of joints-level, perpendicular, or otherwise; and by the aid of cement, iron, lead, or copper; which various operations require much practical dexterity and some skill in geometry and mechanics.

Q - And what by being both, and frequenting sundry Lodges?

A - To act on the square, observe a proper deportment in the Lodge, pay due and becoming respect to the Worshipful Master and his presiding officers, to abstain from all political or religious disputes which might breed dissension among the Brethren, and in time entail a scandal on the Craft.

Q - In what degree in Freemasonry were you initiated?

A - That of an Entered Apprentice.

Q - How long should an Entered Apprentice serve his Master?

A - Seven years is the stipulated time; but less will suffice, if found qualified for preferment.

Q - How should he serve him?

A - With Freedom, Fervency, and Zeal.

Q - Excellent qualities; what are their emblems?

A - Chalk, Charcoal, and Clay.

Q - Why?

A - Nothing is more free than Chalk; the slightest touch leaves a trace. Nothing more fervent than Charcoal; for when properly lighted no metal can resist its force. Nothing more zealous than Clay, our mother Earth; she is continually labouring for our support. Thence we came, and there we must all return.

Q - If you wished to give your son a Masonic name, what would you call him?

A - Lewis.

Q - What does Lewis denote?

A - Strength.

Q. - How is it depicted in our Lodges?

A - By certain pieces of metal dovetailed into a stone, forming a cramp; and when in combination with some of the mechanical powers, such as a system of pulleys, it enables the Operative Mason to raise great weights to certain heights with little encumbrance, and to fix them on their proper bases.

Q - Lewis being the son of a Mason, what is his duty, to his aged parents?

A - To bear the heat and burden of the day, which they by reason of their age, ought to be exempt from; to assist them in time of need, and thereby render the close of their days happy and comfortable.

Q - His privilege for so doing?

A - That of being made a Mason before any other person, however dignified.

Q -Why are we called Freemasons?

A - Because we are free to, and free from.

Q - Free to, and free from what?

A - Free to good fellowship, and ought to be free from vice.

Q - If a Mason of this description were missing, where would you expect to find him?

A - Between the Square and Compasses.

Q - Why there?

A - Because by acting on the one he would be sure to be found within the other.

Q - How would you clothe your Mason?

A - With the distinguishing badge of a Mason.

Q - How do you know a Mason in the day?

A - By seeing him, and observing the Sign.

Q.- How in the night?

A - By receiving the Token, and hearing the Word.

Q - How blows the wind in Freemasonry?

A - Favourably, due East or West.

Q - For what purpose?

A - To cool and refresh men at labour.

Q - It has a further allusion?

A - To that miraculous wind which proved so essential in working the happy deliverance of the children of Israel from their Egyptian bondage.

Q - Why is the wind deemed favourable to Freemasonry in only those particular points of the Compass?

A - When The Great Architect of the Universe thought proper to deliver His chosen people from their Egyptian bondage, He commanded His faithful servant Moses to lead them towards the land of Canaan, which He had promised them for an inheritance: he accordingly conducted them through the desert to the extremity of Egypt, where they encamped for the night on the borders of the Red Sea. Pharaoh, regretting the loss of many useful slaves, gathered together mighty army of horse, foot, and chariots order to bring them back to their for captivity, not doubting of success, as he knew that the Israelites were unarmed and undisciplined, and that their journey was impeded by cattle and baggage. The Israelites, seeing the Red Sea in the front, the impassable mountains on the right and left, and the Egyptian army rapidly advancing in their rear, murmured against their leader, and said. Why hast thou brought us into the wilderness to perish? Was there not ground enough Egypt for our interment? But Moses spoke comfortably to them, and bade them be good cheer; for on that day they should experience the salvation of the Lord. He then, after a fervent prayer to the throne of grace, stretched his sacred rod over Red Sea, which caused a strong east wind to blow, dividing the waters that they stood as a wall on each side, affording Israelites a passage through on dry land Pharaoh seeing this, followed them without hesitation, and already deemed the fugitives within his power, when, in order to check his presumption, the Almighty sent a miraculous pillar of fire and cloud, which had two wonderful effects; the fire gave light to Israelites and facilitated their progress; the cloud proved darkness to Pharaoh and followers, and retarded their march. The Almighty sent a further impediment to the enemy, which was an angel who struck off their chariot-wheels, occasioning them to drag heavily, so that the Egyptian army and the children of Israel came not together. At the dawn of day, Pharaoh, perceiving the hand of the Lord work sorely against him gave order to his troops to discontinue the pursuit, and return by the way they came; but it was then too late, for by that time the Israelites had gained the opposite coast; when Moses bade them look back on their long-dreaded enemies, for from that time forward they should see them no more; he then again stretched his sacred rod over the waters, which caused them to burst their invisible chains, and rush into their primitive channel, overwhelming Pharaoh and all his host. In commemoration of this happy deliverance, the children of Israel went many days' journey into the wilderness, singing psalms and thanksgiving to their Omnipotent deliverer; since which period the wind in due East or West has been deemed favourable to Freemasonry.

Q - What are the distinguishing characteristics of a good Freemason?

A - Virtue, Honour, and Mercy and may they ever be found in a Freemason's breast.

Q - I will thank you to define VIRTUE.

A - In reading the history of ancient Rome, we find that the Consul Marcellus intended to erect a Temple to be dedicated to Virtue and Honour; but being prevented, at .that time, from carrying his design into execution, he afterwards altered his plans, and erected two Temples, contiguous to each other, so situated that the only avenue to the Temple of Honour was through that of Virtue; thereby leaving an elegant moral to posterity, that Virtue is the only direct road to Honour. Virtue is the highest exercise of, and improvement to, reason; the integrity, harmony, and just balance of affection; the health, strength, and beauty of the soul. The perfection of Virtue is to give reason its full scope; to obey the authority of conscience with alacrity; to exercise the defensive talents with fortitude, the public with justice, the private with temperance, and all of them with prudence; that is, in a due proportion to each other, with a calm and diffusive beneficence; to love and adore God with an unrivaled and disinterested affection and to acquiesce in the dispensations of Divine providence with a cheerful resignation. Every approach to this standard is a step towards perfection and happiness, and any deviation therefrom has a tendency to vice and to misery.

Q - HONOUR?

A - May justly be defined to be the spirit and supererogation of Virtue; the true foundation of mutual faith and credit; and the real intercourse by which the business of life is transacted with safety and pleasure. It implies the united sentiments of Virtue, Truth, and justice, carried by a generous mind beyond those mere moral obligations which the laws require, or can punish the violation of. True honour, though a different principle from religion, is that which produces the same effects; the lines of action although drawn from different parts, terminate in the same point. Religion embraces Virtue, as it is enjoined by the laws of God; Honour, as it is graceful and ornamental to human nature. The religious man fears, the man of Honour scorns, to do an ill action; the latter considers vice as something beneath him; the other as something which is offensive to the Divine Being. A true man of Honour will not content himself with the literal discharge of the duties of a man and a citizen; he raises and signifies them to magnanimity: he gives, when he may, with propriety refuse; and forgives, where he may with justice resent. The whole of his conduct is guided by the noblest sentiments of his own unvitiated heart; a true moral rectitude of the uniform rule of his actions; and a just praise and approbation his due reward.

Q - MERCY?

A - Is a refined virtue, and when possessed by the monarch, adds a lustre to every gem that adorns his crown; if by the warrior, it gives an unceasing freshness to the wreath that shades his brow. It is the companion of true honour, and the ameliorator of justice, on whose bench, when enthroned, it interposes a shield of defense on behalf of the victim, impenetrable to the sword. And as the vernal showers descend on the earth, to refresh and invigorate the whole vegetable creation, so mercy, acting on the heart, when the vital fluids are condensed by rancour and revenge, by its exhilarating warmth returns nature to its source in purer streams. It is the peculiar attribute of the Deity, on which the best and wisest of us must rest our hopes and dependence; for at the final day of retribution, when arraigned at His bar, and the actions of this mortal life are unveiled to view, though His justice may demand the fiat, we hope and trust His Mercy will avert the doom.

CHARGE

May Virtue, Honour, and Mercy continue to distinguish Free and Accepted Masons.

THE LECTURE OF THE SECOND DEGREE OF FREEMASONRY

TRACING BOARD—SECOND DEGREE

INTRODUCTORY ADDRESS

Masonry is a progressive science consisting of different Degrees, calculated for the more gradual advancement in the knowledge of its mysteries; according to the progress we make, we limit or extend our inquiries, and in proportion to our capacities, we attain to a greater or lesser degree of perfection. The Lecture of this Degree is divided into five sections, which are devoted to the study of human science, and to tracing the goodness and majesty of the Creator by minutely analysing His works. Throughout the First Degree, virtue is depicted in its most beautiful colours, and the principles of knowledge are impressed on the mind by sensible and lively images; it is therefore considered the best introduction to the Second Degree, which not only extends the same plan but embraces a more diffusive system; from this proceeds a rational amusement, while the mental faculties are fully employed, the judgement is properly exercised, a spirit of emulation prevails, and each vies as to who shall excel in promulgating the valuable principles of the institution.

SECTION ONE

Q - Where were you passed to the Degree of a Fellow Craft?

A - In a Lodge of Fellow Crafts.

Q - Consisting of how many?

A - Five.

Q - Under what denominations?

A - The Worshipful Master his two Wardens, and two Fellow Crafts.

Q - How got you passed?

A - By undergoing a previous examination in open Lodge, and being intrusted with a test of merit leading to that degree.

Q - Where were you then conducted?

A - To a convenient room, adjoining a Fellow Craft's Lodge, for the purpose of being prepared.

Q - How were you prepared?

A - In a manner somewhat similar to the former, save that in this degree I was not hoodwinked, my left arm, breast, and right knee were made bare., and my left heel. was slipshod.

Q - What enabled you to, claim admission into a Fellow Craft's Lodge?

A - The help of God, the assistance of the Square, and the benefit of a Passing Word.

Q - How did you gain admission?

A - By the knocks of an Entered Apprentice.

Q - On what were you admitted?

A - The Square.

Q - What is a Square?

A - An angle of 90 degrees, or the fourth part of a circle.

Q - What are the peculiar objects of research in this degree?

A - The hidden mysteries of nature and science.

Q - When admitted into the Lodge, how were you disposed of?

A - I was conducted between the Deacons to the left of the Senior Warden and directed to advance as a Mason.

Q - What were you then desired to do?

A - Kneel, and receive the benefit of a Masonic prayer.

Q - Which I will thank you for.

A - We supplicate the continuance of Thine aid, O merciful Lord, on behalf of ourselves and him who kneels before Thee; may the work begun in Thy name be continued to Thy Glory, and evermore established in us, by obedience to Thy precepts.

So mote it be.

Q - After the recital of this prayer, how were you disposed of?.

A - I was conducted twice round the Lodge.

Q - What was required of you the first time?

A - To salute the Worship Master as a Mason, advance to the Junior Warden as such, showing the Sign and communicating the Token and Word.

Q - What were the Brethren then called on to observe?

A - That I, who had been regularly initiated into Freemasonry, was about to pass in view before them, to show that I was the candidate properly prepared to be passed to the degree of a Fellow Craft.

Q - What was required of you the second time?

A - To salute the Worshipful Master and Junior Warden as a Mason, advance to the Senior Warden. as such, showing the sign and communicating the pass grip and Pass Word leading from the First to the Second Degree.

Q - How did the Senior Warden then proceed?

A - He presented me to the Worshipful Master, as a candidate properly prepared to be passed to the Second Degree.

Q - What did the Master then order?

A - The Senior Warden to direct the Senior Deacon to instruct me to advance to the East in due form.

Q - I will thank you to show the method of advancing from West to East in this degree.

A - (It is done.)

Q - When placed before the Master in the East how did he address you?

A - As in every case the degrees in Freemasonry are to be kept separate and distinct, another Obligation will now be required of you, in many respects similar to the former, are you willing to take it? To which I gave my assent.

Q - What did the Master then desire you to do?

A - Kneel on my right knee, my left foot formed in a square, place my right hand on the Volume of the Sacred Law, while my left arm was supported in the angle of the Square.

Q - In that attitude what were you about to do?

A - Take the Solemn Obligation of a Fellow Craft.

Q - Which I will thank you for.

A - I, A. B., in the presence of the Grand Geometrician of the Universe, and of this worthy and worshipful Lodge of Fellow Craft Freemasons, regularly held, assembled, and properly dedicated, of my own free will and accord, do hereby and hereon solemnly promise and swear, that I will always hele, conceal, and never improperly reveal any or either of the secret or mysteries of or belonging to the Second Degree in Freemasonry, denominated the Fellow-Craft's, to him who is but an Entered Apprentice, any more than I would either of them to the uninstructed and popular world who are not Masons. I further solemnly pledge myself to act as a true and faithful craftsman, answer signs, obey summonses, and maintain the principles inculcated in the former Degree; these several points I solemnly swear to observe, without evasion, equivocation, or mental reservation of any kind, under no less a penalty, on the violation of any of them, than that of having, chest ripped open, my heart torn out and thrown as carrion to the revenging beasts of the field and the air. So help me, Almighty God, and keep me steadfast in this my Solemn Obligation of a Fellow Craft Freemason.

Q - Having taken the Solemn Obligation of a Fellow Craft, what did the Master require of you?

A - As a pledge of my fidelity, and to render this a solemn Obligation, which might otherwise be considered but a serious promise, to seal it with my lips twice on the Volume of the Sacred Law.

Q - How did he then address you?

A - Your progress in Masonry is marked by the position of the Square and Compasses. When you were made an Entered Apprentice both points were hid; in this degree one is disclosed, implying that you are now in the midway of Freemasonry, superior to an Entered Apprentice, but inferior to that to which I trust you will hereafter attain.

Q - How did the Master then proceed?

A - He friendly took me by the right hand and said, Rise, newly Obligated Fellow Craft Freemason.

Q - How did he then address you?

A - Having taken the Solemn Obligation of a Fellow Craft, I shall proceed to intrust you with the secrets of the degree. You will therefore advance to me as at your Initiation.

Q - What did the Master then direct you to do?

A - Take another step towards him with my left foot bringing the right heel into its hollow as before; that, he informed me, is the second regular step in Freemasonry, and it is in this position that the secrets of the degree are communicated.

Q - Of what do those Secrets consist?

A - As in the former instance, of a Sign, Token, and Word, with this difference, that in this degree the Sign is of a three fold nature.

Q - I will thank you for the first part of the three fold sign.

A - (Which is given.)

Q - What is that?

A - The Sign of Fidelity emblematically to shield the repository of my secrets from the attacks of the insidious.

Q - The second part.

A - (Which is given.)

Q - What is that?

A - The Hailing Sign or Sign of Prayer.

Q - When did it take its rise?

A - This is said to have been the Sign used by Joshuah when fighting the battles of the Lord "in the going down to Beth-horon." In this position he spake those memorable words, "Sun, stand thou still upon Gibeon; and thou, Moon, in the valley of Ajalon." And the sun stood still, and the moon stayed, until the people had avenged themselves upon their enemies.

Q - The third part?

A - (Which is given.)

Q - What is that?

A - The Penal Sign.

Q - To what does it allude?

A - The Penalty of my Obligation implying that as a man of honour, and a Fellow Craft Freemason, I would rather, have my chest ripped open and my heart torn out and thrown to the revenging beasts of the field rather than betray any secret or secrets, mystery or mysteries of this the Second Degree of Freemasonry.

Q - Communicate the Token to me.

A - (Which is done.)

Q - Is that correct?

A - It is, Right Worshipful Master.

Q - What does that demand?

A - A Word.

Q - Give me that Word.

A - I was taught to be cautious in this degree as well as in the former. I will letter or halve it with you.

Q - Do which you please, and begin.

A - (Which is done.)

Q - Whence is this Word derived?

A - From the right hand pillar at the entrance or porch of King Solomon's Temple, so named after the Great High Priest who officiated at its dedication.

Q - The import of the Word?

A - To establish.

Q - And what when conjoined with that in the former degree?

A - Stability For God said "In strength will I establish my word in this mine house that it will stand firm forever".

Q - Having been Obligated and intrusted, were you invested?

A - I was, with the distinguishing badge of a Fellow Craft Free-mason, which the Senior Warden informed me was to mark the progress I had made in the science.

Q - Repeat the address you then received from the Master.

A - Let me add to what has been stated by the Senior Warden, that the badge with which you have now been invested, points out that, as a Craftsman, you are expected to make the liberal arts and sciences your future study, that you may the better be enabled to discharge your duties as a Mason, and estimate the wonderful works of the Almighty.

Q - Where were you then ordered to be placed?

A - At the South East part of the Lodge.

Q - Repeat the charge.

A - Masonry being a progressive science, when you were made an Entered Apprentice you were placed at the North East part of the Lodge, to show that you were newly admitted; you are now placed at the South East part, to mark the progress you have made in the science; you now stand, to all external appearance, a just and upright Fellow Craft Freemason, and I give it you in strong terms of recommendation ever to continue, and act as such; and, as I trust the import of the former charge neither is, nor ever will be, effaced from your memory, I shall content myself with observing, that as in the previous degree you made yourself acquainted with the principles of moral truth and virtue, you are now permitted to extend your researches into the hidden mysteries of nature and science.

Q - What did the Master then present to you?

A - The working tools of a Fellow Craft Freemason, which are the Square, Level, and Plumb Rule.

Q - Their uses?

A - The Square is to try, and adjust rectangular corners of buildings, and assist in bringing rude matter into due form; the Level to lay levels and prove horizontals; the Plumb Rule to try, and adjust uprights while fixing them on their proper bases.

Q - But as we are not all Operative Masons, but rather Free and Accepted, or speculative, how do we apply these tools to our morals?

A - In this sense, the Square teaches morality, the Level equality, and the Plumb Rule justness and uprightness of life and actions. Thus by square conduct, level steps, and upright intentions, we hope to ascend to those immortal mansions, whence all goodness emanates.

Q - What permission did you then receive?

A - To retire, in order. to restore myself to my personal comforts, and the Worshipful Master informed me, that on my return to the Lodge he would call my attention to an explanation of the Tracing Board.

CHARGE

All just and upright Fellow Craft Freemasons.

SECTION TWO

Q - Why were you passed to the degree of a Fellow Craft?

A - For the sake of Geometry or the fifth science, on which Masonry is founded.

Q - What is Geometry?

A - A science whereby we find out the contents of bodies unmeasured by comparing them with those already measured.

Q - Its proper subjects?

A - Magnitude and Extension, or a regular progression of science from a point to a line, from a line to a superficies, and from a superficies to a solid.

Q - What is a point?

A - The beginning of geometrical matter.

Q - A line?

A - The continuation of the same.

Q - A superficies?

A - Length and breadth without a given thickness.

Q - A solid?

A - Length and breadth with a given thickness, which forms a cube, and comprehends a whole.

Q - Where was Geometry founded as a science?

A - At Alexandria in Egypt.

Q - How came it to be founded there?

A - The River Nile annually overflowing its banks, caused the inhabitants to retire to the high and mountainous parts of the country. When the waters subsided they returned to their former habitations; but the floods frequently washing away their landmarks, caused grievous disputes among them, which often terminated in a civil war. They hearing of a Fellowcraft's Lodge being held at Alexandria, the capital of their country, where Euclid presided, a deputation of the inhabitants repaired thither, and laid their grievances before him. He with the assistance of his Wardens and the rest of the Brethren, gathered together the scattered elements of Geometry, digested, arranged, and brought them into a regular system, such as was practised by most nations in those days, but is bettered in the present by the use of fluxions, conic sections, and other improvements. By the science of Geometry he taught the Egyptians to measure and ascertain the different districts of land; by that means put an end to their quarrels: and amicably terminated their differences.

Q - I will thank you for the moral advantages of Geometry.

A - Geometry, the first and noblest of sciences, is the basis on which the superstructure of Masonry is erected. By Geometry we may curiously trace nature through her various windings to her most concealed recesses. By it we may discover the power, wisdom, and goodness of the Grand Geometrician of the Universe, and view with amazing delight the beautiful proportions which connect and grace this vast machine. By it we may discover how the planets move in their different orbits, and mathematically demonstrate their various revolutions. By it we may rationally account for the return of seasons, and the mixed variety of scenes which each season produces to the discerning eye. Numberless worlds are around us, all formed by the same Divine artist, which roll through the vast expanse, and are conducted by the same unerring law of nature. While such objects engage our attention, how must we improve, and with what grand ideas must such knowledge fill our minds! It was a survey of nature, and an observation of her beautiful proportions, which first induced men to imitate the Divine plan, and study symmetry and order. This gave rise to society, and birth to every useful art. The architect began to design and the plans which he laid down having been improved by time and experience, have produced some of those excellent works which have been the admiration every age.

Q - Did you ever travel?

A - My forefathers did.

Q - Where did they travel?

A - Due East and West.

Q - What was the object of their travels?

A - They travelled East in search of instruction, and West to propagate the knowledge they had gained.

Q - Did you ever work?

A - My ancient Brethren did.

Q - Where did they work?

A - At the building of King Solomon's Temple and many other stately edifices.

Q - If they worked, I presume they received wages? How long first?

A - Six days or less.

Q - Why not on the seventh?

A - Because the Almighty was pleased be six days, periodically, in creating the Heavens and the Earth, and all that is therein and thereon contained; and rested on the seventh.

Q - A beautiful Illustration of the periods of the creation, I will thank you for.

A - When we consider that the formation of the world was work of that Omnipotent being who created this beautiful system of the Universe, and caused all nature to be under His immediate care and protection, how ought we to magnify and adore His Holy name, for His infinite wisdom, goodness, and mercy to the children of men! Before it pleased the Almighty to command this vast whole into existence, the elements and materials of Creation lay blended together without form or distinction. Darkness was over the great deep, when the Spirit of God moved on the face of the waters. And as an example to man, that things of moment ought to be done with due deliberation, He was pleased to be six days, periodically, in commanding it from chaos to perfection.

The first instance of His supreme power was made manifest by commanding Light. Being pleased with the operation of His divine goodness, He gave it His sacred approbation; and distinguished it by a name; the light He called day, and the darkness He called night.

In order to keep this new-framed matter within just limits, He employed the second period in laying the foundation of the Heavens; which He called firmament; designed to keep the waters within the clouds and those beneath them asunder.

The third period was employed in commanding these waters into due bounds on the retreat of which, dry land appeared which He called Earth; and the gathering together of the mighty waters He called Seas. The Earth being as yet irregular and uncultivated God spake the word, and it was immediately covered with a beautiful carpet of grass, designed as pasture for the brute creation; to which succeeded herbs, plan flowers, shrubs, and trees of all sorts, to full growth, maturity, and perfection.

On the fourth period, those two grand luminaries, the Sun and Moon, were created one to rule the day, and the other to govern the night. The sacred historian further informs us they were ordained for signs and for seasons, for days and years. Besides the Sun and Moon, the Almighty was pleased to bespangle the ethereal concave with a multitude of Stars, that man, who He intended to make, might contemplate thereon, and justly admire the majesty and glory of His creator.

On the fifth period, He created the birds to fly in the air, that man might please both his eyes and ears; by being delighted with some for their beautiful plumage and uncommon instincts; and with others for their melodious notes. He also in the same period caused the waters to bring forth variety of fish; and to impress man with reverential awe of His Divine omnipotence. He created great whales; which, with other inhabitants of the deep, after their kin multiplied and increased exceedingly.

On the sixth period, he created the beasts of the field, and the reptiles that crawl the earth. And here we may plainly perceive the wisdom and goodness of the Almighty, made manifest in all His proceedings, by producing what effects He pleased, without the aid of natural causes; such. as giving light to the world before He created the Sun; and causing the earth to become fruitful without the influence of the Heavenly Bodies. He did not create the beasts of the field until He had provided them with sufficient herbage for their support; nor did He make man until He had completed the rest of His works and finished and furnished him a dwelling, with everything requisite both for life and pleasure. Then, still more to dignify the work of His hands, He created man; who came into the world with greater splendour than any creature which had preceded him; they coming into existence by no other than a single command, God spake the word, and it was done, but at the formation of man there was a consultation. God expressly said, Let us make man: who was accordingly formed out of the dust of the earth; the breath of life was breathed into his nostrils, and man became a living soul. In this one creature was amassed whatever is excellent in the whole creation; the quality or substance of an animal being; the life of plants; the sense of beasts; and above all the understanding of Angels; created after the immediate image of God, with the rectitude of body; intimating thereby that integrity, and uprightness, should ever influence him to adore his Benign Creator, who had so liberally bestowed on him the faculty of speech, and endued him with that noble instinct called reason.

The Almighty, as His last, best gift to man, then created woman; under His forming hands a creature grew, manlike, but different sex, so lovely fair, that what seemed fair in all the world, seemed now mean, or in her summed up, in her contained. On she came, led by her heavenly Maker, though unseen, and guided by His voice; adorned with what all earth or Heaven could bestow to make her amiable; grace was in all her steps, Heaven in her eye, in every gesture dignity and love. On the sixth period God's works being ended, on the seventh He rested from His labour; He therefore sanctified, blessed, and hallowed the seventh day; thereby teaching men a useful lesson; to work six days industriously in support of themselves and families; strictly commanding them to rest on the seventh, the better to contemplate on the works of the creation, and adore Him as their Creator; to go into His sanctuary to return Him thanks for their preservation, well-being, and all the other blessings they have so liberally received at His hands.

CHARGE

May a remembrance of the Six Periods of the Creation stimulate Fellow Crafts to acts of industry.

SECTION THREE

Q - What were the names of the two great Pillars which were placed at the Porch or Entrance of King Solomon's Temple?

A - That on the left was called Boaz, and that on the right Jachin.

Q - What are their separate and conjoint significant?

A - The former denotes strength the latter to establish and when conjoined stability, for God said in strength will I establish my word in the Mine house that it will stand fast forever.

Q - The height of those Pillars?

A - Seventeen cubits and a half each.

Q - Their circumference?

A - Twelve.

Q - Their diameter?

A - Four.

Q - Were they formed hollow or solid?

A - Hollow.

Q - Why were they formed hollow?

A - The better to serve as Archives to Masonry, for therein were deposited the constitutional rolls.

Q - Being, formed hollow, what was the thickness of the outer rim or shell?

A - Four inches, or a hand's breadth.

Q - What were they made of?

A - Molten brass.

Q - Where were they cast?

A - In the plain of Jordan, in the clay ground between Succoth and Zeredathah where King Solomon ordered those and all his holy vessels to be cast.

Q - Who superintended the casting?

A - Hiram Abif.

Q - What were they adorned with?

A - Two Chapiters.

Q - The height of those Chapiters?

A - Five cubits each.

Q - What were they enriched with?

A - Net-work, Lily-work, and Pomegranates.

Q - What do Net-work, Lily-work, and Pomegranates denote?

A - Net-work, from the connection of its meshes, denotes unity; Lily-work, from its whiteness, peace; and Pomegranates, from the exuberance of their seed, denote plenty.

Q - How many rows of Pomegranates were there on each Chapiter, and how many in a row?

A - There were two rows of Pomegranates on each Chapiter, one hundred in a row.

Q - What were they further adorned with?

A - Two Spherical Balls.

Q - What were delineated thereon?

A - Maps of the Celestial and Terrestrial Globes.

Q - What does that point out?

A - Masonry universal.

Q - When were they considered finished?

A - When the net-work or canopy was thrown over them.

Q - Where were they ordered to be placed?

A - At the Entrance of the Temple as a memorial to the children of Israel of that miraculous pillar of fire and cloud, which had two wonderful effects: the fire gave light to the Israelites during their escape from their Egyptian bondage and the cloud proved darkness to Pharaoh and his followers when they attempted to overtake them. King Solomon ordered them to be placed at the entrance of the Temple, as the most proper and conspicuous situation for the children of Israel to have the happy deliverance of their forefathers continually before their eyes, in going to and returning from, Divine Worship.

Q - Where did our Ancient Brethren go to receive their wages?

A - Into the Middle Chamber of King Solomon's Temple.

Q - How did they get there?

A - By the Porch or Entrance on the South side.

Q - Having entered the Porch, where did they arrive?

A - At the foot of the winding staircase, which led to the Middle Chamber.

Q - Who opposed their ascent?

A - The Junior Warden.

Q - What did he demand of our Antient Brethren?

A - The Pass Grip and Pass Word leading from the first to the second degree.

Q - Communicate the Pass Grip to me.

A - (Which is done.)

Q - Is that correct?

A - It is.

Q - What does that demand?

A - A Pass Word.

Q - Give me that Pass Word.

A - (Which is given.)

Q - What does this word denote?

A - Plenty.

Q - How is it depicted in our Lodges?

A - By an Ear of Corn near to a pool of Water.

Q - I will thank you for the origin of the word.

A - The word dates its origin from the time that an army of Ephraimites crossed the river Jordan in a hostile manner against Jephtha, the renowned Gileaditish general; the reason they assigned for this unfriendly visit was, that they had not been called out to partake of the honours of the Ammonitish war, but their true aim was to partake of the rich spoils with which, in consequence of that war, Jephtha: and his army were then laden. The Ephraimites had always been considered a clamorous and turbulent people, but then broke out into open violence, and after many severe taunts to the Gileadites in general, threatened to destroy their victorious commander and his house with fire. Jephtha, on his part, tried all lenient means to appease them, but finding these ineffectual, had recourse to rigorous ones; he therefore drew out his army, gave the Ephraimites battle, defeated, and put them to flight, and to render his victory decisive, and to secure himself from like molestation in future, he sent detachments of his army to secure the passages of the river Jordan, over which he knew the insurgents must of necessity attempt to go, in order to regain their own country, giving strict orders to his guards, that if a fugitive came that way, owning himself an Ephraimite, he should immediately be slain; but if he prevaricated, or said nay, a test Word was to be put to him to pronounce, the Word, they, from a defect in aspiration peculiar to their dialect, could not pronounce it properly, but called it something which small variation discovered their country, and cost them their lives; and Scripture informs us that there fell on that day, on the field of battle and on the banks of the Jordan, forty and two thousand Ephraimites. And as this word was then a test word to distinguish friend from foe, King Solomon afterwards caused it to be adopted as a Pass Word in a Fellow Craft's Lodge, to prevent any unqualified person ascending the winding staircase, which led to the Middle Chamber of the Temple.

CHARGE

May Peace, Plenty, and Unanimity ever subsist among Fellow Crafts.

SECTION FOUR

Q - After our ancient Brethren had given those convincing proofs to the Junior Warden, what did he say to them?

A - Pass.

Q - Where did they then pass?

A - Up the winding staircase.

Q - Consisting of how many Steps?

A - Three, five, seven, or more.

Q - Why three?

A - It takes three to rule a lodge.

Q - Why five?

A - To hold a lodge.

Q -Why seven or more?

A - To make a lodge perfect.

Q - Who are the three that Rule a Lodge?

A - The Worshipful Master and his two Wardens.

Q - Who are the five that hold a Lodge?

A - The Worshipful Master, two Wardens, and two Fellow Crafts.

Q - Who are the seven that make it perfect?

A - Two Entered Apprentices added to the former five.

Q - Why do three Rule a Lodge?

A - Because there were but three Grand Masters who bore sway at the building of the first Temple at Jerusalem., namely, Solomon King of Israel, Hiram King of Tyre, and Hiram Abif.

Q - Why do five hold a Lodge?

A - In allusion to the five noble orders of Architecture, namely, the Tuscan, Doric, Ionic, Corinthian, and Composite.

Q - I will thank you for the rise of those orders.

A - In the history of man, there is nothing more remarkable than that Masonry and civilisation, like twin sisters, have gone hand in hand. The Orders of Architecture mark their growth and progress. Dark, dreary, and comfortless were those days when Masonry had not laid her line, or extended her compass. The race of mankind, in full possession of wild and savage liberty, mutually afraid of, and offending each other, hid themselves in thickets of the wood, or in dens and caverns of the earth. In those poor recesses and gloomy solitudes, Masonry found them, and the Grand Geometrician of the Universe, pitying their forlorn situation, instructed them to build houses for their case, defence, and comfort. It is easy to conceive that in the early state of society, genius had expanded but little. The first efforts were small, and the structure simple and rude; no more than a number of trees leaning together at the top, in the form of a cone, interwoven with twigs, and plastered with mud to exclude the air and complete the work.

In this early period we may suppose each desirous to render his own habitation more convenient than his neighbour's, by improving on what had already been done. Thus in time, observation, assisting that natural sagacity inherent even in un-cultivated minds, led them to consider the inconveniences of the round sort of habitation, and to build others, more spa-cious and convenient, of the square form, by placing trunks of trees perpendicularly in the ground to form the sides, fill-ing the interstices between them with the branches, closely woven, and covered with clay. Horizontal beams were then placed on the upright trunks, which being strongly joined at the angles, kept the sides firm, and likewise served to support the covering or roof of the building, composed of joists, on which were laid several beds of reeds, leaves, and clay.

Yet, rough and inelegant as these buildings were, they had this salutary effect; that by aggregating mankind together, they led the way to new improvements in arts and civilisation; for the hardest bodies will polish by collision, the roughest manners by communion and intercourse. Thus, by degrees, mankind improved in the art of building, and invented methods to make their huts more lasting and handsome, as well as convenient. They took off the bark and other uneven-ness from the trunks of the trees that formed the sides; raised them above the earth and humidity, on stones; and covered each of them with a flat stone or tile to keep off the rain. The spaces between the ends of the joists they closed with clay or some other substance; and the ends of the joists they covered with boards, cut in the manner of triglyphs, The form of the roof was likewise altered; for, being, on account its flatness, unfit to throw off the rain that fell in abundance during the winter seasons, they raised it in the middle, giving it the form of a gable roof by placing rafters on the joists to support the clay, and other materials, that composed the covering.

From these simple forms the Orders of Architecture took their rise; for when buildings of wood were set aside, and men began erect solid and stately edifices of stone, they, imitated the parts necessity had introduced into the primitive huts, and adapted them in the Temples; which, although at first simple and rude, were in course of time, and by the ingenuity of succeeding architects, wrought and improved to such a degree of perfection on different models, that each was by way of eminence denominated an "Order."

Of the Orders: Three are of Grecian origin, and are called Grecian Orders. They are distinguished by the names of the Doric, Ionic, and Corinthian; and exhibit three distinct characters of composition suggested by the diversity of form in the human frame. The other two are of Italian origin, and are called Roman Orders; they are distinguished by the names of the Tuscan and Composite.

The Tuscan Order is the simplest and most solid, and is placed first in the list of the five Orders of Architecture on account of its plainness. Its column is seven diameters high; the base, capital, and entablature have but few mouldings, and no other ornaments. Whence it has been compared to a sturdy labourer dressed in homely apparel. This Order is no other than the Doric, more simplified or deprived of its ornaments to suit certain purposes; and adapted by the inhabitants of Tuscany, who were a colony of the Dorians. Yet there is a peculiar beauty in its simplicity, which adds to its value, and renders it fit to be used in structures where the rich and more delicate Orders might be deemed superfluous.

The Doric is the first of the Grecian Orders, and is placed second in the list of the five Orders of Architecture. Its column, agreeable to modem proportions, is eight diameters high. It has no ornament except mouldings on either base or capital. Its frieze is distinguished by triglyphs and metopes, and its cornice by mutules. Being the most ancient of all the orders, it retains more of the primitive-hut style in its form than any of the rest. The triglyphs in the frieze represent the ends of the joists, and the mutules in its cornice represent the rafters. The composition of this Order is both grand and noble; being formed after the model of a muscular, full-grown man, delicate ornaments are repugnant to its characteristic solidity. It therefore succeeds best in the regularity of its proportions; and is principally used in warlike structures where strength and a noble simplicity are required.

At this era, their buildings, although admirably calculated for strength and convenience, wanted something in grace and elegance, which a continual observation of the softer sex supplied; for the eye that is charmed with symmetry must be conscious of woman's elegance and beauty. This gave rise to the Ionic Order. its column is nine diameters high; its capital is adorned with volutes, and its cornice has dentils. History informs us that the famous Temple of Diana, at Ephesus (which was upwards of two hundred years in building), was composed of this Order. Both elegance and ingenuity were displayed in the invention of this column. It is formed after the model of a beautiful young woman, of an elegant shape, dressed in her hair, as a contrast to that of the Doric, which represents a strong robust man. Thus the human genius began to bud; the leaf and flower ripening to perfection, producing the fairest and finest fruits, every liberal art, every ingenious science, which could civilise, refine, and exalt mankind. Then it was that Masonry put on her richest robes and decked herself in her most gorgeous apparel. A new capital was in vented at Corinth by Calimachus, which gave rise to the Corinthian, which is deemed the richest of the Orders, and masterpiece of art. Its column is ten diameters high, its capital is adorned with two rows of leaves, and eight volutes which sustain the abacus. This order is chiefly used in stately and superb structures. Calimachus took the hint of the capital of this column from the following remarkable circumstance. Accidentally passing the tomb of a young lady, he perceived a basket of toys which had been left there by her nurse, covered with a tile, and placed over an Acanthus root; as the leaves grew up, they encompassed the basket, till arriving at the tile, they met with an obstruction and bent downwards; Calimachis, struck with the object, set about imitating the, figure; the base of the capital he made to represent the basket, the abacus the tile; and the volutes the bending leaves.

Yet not content with this utmost production of her own powers, Masonry held forth her torch and illumined the whole circle of arts and sciences. This gave rise to the Composite Order, so named from being composed of parts of the other Orders. It capital is adorned with the two rows of leaves of the Corinthian, the volutes of the Ionic; and has the quarter-round of the Tuscan and Doric Orders. Its column is ten diameters high; and its cornice has dentils or simple modillions. This Order is chiefly used in structures where strength, elegance, and beauty are displayed.

Painting and Sculpture strained every nerve to decorate the buildings fair science had raised; while the curious hand designed the furniture and tapestry, beautifying and adorning them with music, ELOQUENCE, POETRY, TEMPERANCE, FORTITUDE, PRUDENCE, JUSTICE, VIRTUE, HONOUR,

MERCY, FAITH, HOPE, CHARITY, and many other Masonic emblems, but none shone with greater splendour than BROTHERLY LOVE, RELIEF, AND TRUTH.

Q - Why do seven or more make a perfect Lodge?

A - Because King Solomon was seven years and upwards, in building, completing, and dedicating the Temple at Jerusalem to God's service.

Q - They have a further allusion?

A - To the seven liberal arts and sciences, viz.: Grammar, Rhetoric, Logic, Arithmetic, Geometry, Music, and Astronomy.

Q - I will thank you to define GRAMMAR.

A - Grammar teaches the proper arrangement of words according to the idiom or dialect of any particular kingdom or people and that excellence of pronunciation which enable us to speak and write a language with accuracy and precision; agreeable to reason, authority, and the strict rules of literature.

Q - RHETORIC?

A - Teaches us to speak copiously and fluently on any subject; not merely with precision alone, but with all the advantages of force and elegance, wisely contriving to captivate the hearers by strength of argument and beauty of expression, whether it be to instruct, exhort, admonish, or applaud.

Q - LOGIC?

A - Teaches us to guide our reason discretionally in the general knowledge of things and to direct our inquiries after truth; as well for the instruction of others as our own improvement. It consists of regular trains of argument, whence we infer, deduce, and conclude, according to certain premises laid down, admitted or granted. In it are employed the faculties of conceiving, reasoning, judging, and disposing;- all of which are naturally led on from one gradation to another, until the point in question is finally determined.

Q - ARITHMETIC?

A - Teaches the powers and properties of numbers; by means of letters, tables, figures, and instruments. By this art, reasons and. demonstrations are given for finding any certain number; whose relation, or affinity, to another number is already discovered.

Q - GEOMETRY?

A - Treats of the powers and properties magnitude in general, where length, length and breadth, or length, breadth, and thickness are considered. By this science, the Architect is able to execute his plans, and estimate his designs; the General to arrange his soldier, the Engineer to mark out ground for encampments; the Geographer to give the dimensions of the world, to delineate the extent of seas, and specify the division of empires, kingdoms, and provinces. By it also the Astronomer is enabled to make his observations, to calculate and fix the duration of times, seasons, years, and cycles; in fine, Geometry is the foundation and root of the mathematics.

Q - MUSIC?

A - Teaches us the art of forming concords, so as to produce a delightful harmony by a mathematical and proportionate arrangement of acute, grave, and mixed sound This art by a variety of experiments is reduced to a demonstrative science, with respect to tones and the intervals of sound. It inquires into the nature of concords and discord and enables us to find out a due proportion between them by numbers; -and is never employed to such advantage as in the praise of The Great Geometrician of the Universe.

Q - ASTRONOMY?

A - Is that Divine art by which we a taught to read the Wisdom, Strength, and Beauty, of the Almighty Creator, in the sacred pages of the Celestial hemisphere. Assisted by Astronomy, we can observe the motions, measure the distances, comprehend the magnitude, and calculate the periods and Eclipses of the Heavenly Bodies; by it also we learn the use of the Globes, the system of the World, and the primary laws of Nature; and while we are employed in the study of this science, we may perceive unparalleled instances of wisdom and goodness, and on every hand may trace the Glorious Author by His works.

CHARGE

May the study of the Seven Liberal Arts and Sciences ever render us susceptible to the benignity of a Supreme Being.

SECTION FIVE

Q - After our ancient Brethren. had gained the summit of the winding staircase, where did they arrive?

A - At the door of the Middle Chamber of the Temple.

Q - How did they find that door?

A - Open, but properly tyled.

Q - Whom. was it tyled by?

A - The Senior Warden.

Q - Whom against?

A - All under the degree of a Fellow Craft.

Q - What did he demand of our ancient Brethren?

A - The Sign, Token, and Word of a Fellow Craft.

Q - After they had given him those convincing proofs, what did he say to them?

A - Pass.

Q - Where did they then pass?

A - Into the Middle Chamber of the Temple.

Q - What did they go there to do?

A - Receive their wages.

Q - How did they receive them?

A - Without scruple or diffidence.

Q - Why in this peculiar manner?

A - Without scruple, well knowing the were justly entitled to them; and without diffidence, from the great reliance they placed on the integrity of their employers in those days.

Q - Before we proceed to finish the Lecture, I wish to be informed into how many classes the workmen were divided.

A - King Solomon divided the various artificers into three classes, a circumstance particularly marked by Masons, as it is from the plans of that monarch to carry on this magnificent structure, we deduce the origin of our present system of government.

Q - Name the classes.

A - Rulers or general directors, Overseer or comforters of the people, and Craftsmen or executors of the work.

Q - Name the number in each class.

A - There were three hundred Rulers. three thousand three hundred Overseers, and eighty thousand Craftsmen. The Rulers and Overseers were all skilled Craftsmen, or men of science. For the purpose of instructing and dividing the employment of the Craftsmen, they were arranged into companies or Lodges, consisting of seven Entered Apprentices. and five Fellow Crafts, and over each Lodge a skilled Craftsman presided.

Q - Why this division?

A - Because this triple division, besides being symbolic, was best calculated to ensure promotion to merit, preserve due subordination, and prevent confusion in the work.

Q - Were there any others employed in the building?

A - There were seventy thousand others employed, consisting of men of burden and hewers of stone, under the superintendence of Adoniram, an ingenious artist, who by his zeal and fidelity arrived at the highest honours, so that the total number of men employed in the building, was one hundred and fifty-three thousand six hundred.

Q - How long were they employed?

A - Seven years and six months, as the work was begun in the fourth year of the reign of King Solomon, on the second day of the second month, and was completed in the eleventh year of his reign. In the following year it was dedicated to God by King Solomon in the presence of the twelve tribes of Israel, and an immense concourse of spectators from the surrounding nations, with all the splendour and magnificence which the ingenuity of man could devise, to acknowledge the goodness and display the glory of his Creator. The prayer used on that solemn occasion is still extant in the sacred records.

Q - When our Ancient Brethren were in the middle Chamber of the Temple, to what was their attention peculiarly drawn?

A - Certain Hebrew characters, which are now depicted in a Fellow Craft's Lodge by the letter G.

Q - What does that letter G denote?

A - God, the Grand Geometrician of the Universe; to whom we must all submit; and whom we ought humbly to adore.

CHARGE

The M.W. Grand M.

THE LECTURE OF THE THIRD DEGREE OF FREEMASONRY

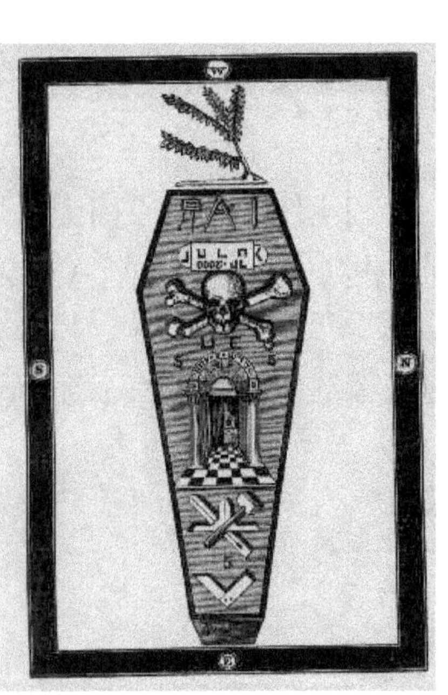

INTRODUCTORY ADDRESS

BRETHREN, every degree of Masonry is progressive, and cannot be attained but by time, patience, and assiduity. In the First Degree, we are taught the duties we owe to God, to our neighbour, and to ourselves. In the Second Degree, we are admitted to participate in the mysteries of human science, and to trace the goodness and majesty of the Creator, by minutely analysing His works. But the Third Degree is the cement of the whole; it is calculated to bind men together by mystic points of fellowship, as in a bond of fraternal affection and brotherly love; it points to the darkness of death and to the obscurity of the grave as the forerunner of a more brilliant light, which shall follow at the resurrection of the just, when these mortal bodies which have been long slumbering in the dust shall be awakened, reunited to their kindred spirit, and clothed with immortality. Among the Brethren of this Degree the ancient Landmarks of the Order are preserved, and it is from them we derive that fund of information, which none but ingenious and expert Masons can supply, whose judgment has been matured by years and experience. To a perfect knowledge of this Degree few attain, but it is an infallible truth, that he who gains by merit those marks of pre-eminence and distinction which the Degree affords, receives a reward which amply compensates for all his attention and assiduity. From the Brethren of this Degree the rules of the Craft are selected, as it is only from those who are capable of giving instruction that we can expect properly to receive it. The Third Lecture, divested of those duties and ceremonies which appertain to the Installation of the R.W.M. and his officers, is divided into three sections, and throughout the whole we are taught to circumscribe our conduct within the limits of the boundary line of our duty to God and man; and by practising out of the Lodge that which we are taught in it we shall convince the world that the principles of Masonry are pure and its requirements just Having premised this much by way of introduction to the Third Lecture, I shall now proceed to inquire of you.

SECTION ONE

Q - Where were you raised to the sublime degree of a Master Mason?

A - In a Lodge of Master Masons.

Q - Consisting of how many?

A - Three.

Q - Under what denominations?

A - The Right Worshipful Master and his two Wardens.

Q - How got you raised?

A - By undergoing a previous examination in open Lodge, and being intrusted with a test of merit leading to that degree.

Q - Where were you then conducted?

A - To a convenient room adjoining a Master Mason's. Lodge, for the purpose of being prepared.

Q - How were you prepared?

A - By having both arms, both breasts, and both knees made bare, and both heels slipshod.

Q What enabled you to claim admission into a Master Mason's. Lodge?

A - The help of God, the united aid of the Square and Compasses, and the benefit of a Passing Word.

Q - How did you gain admission?

A - By the Knocks of a Fellow Craft.

Q - On what were you admitted?

A - Both Points of the Compasses presented to both breasts.

Q - On your admission into the Lodge did you observe anything different from its usual appearance?

A - I did; all was Darkness, save a glimmer of light in the East.

Q - To what does that Darkness allude?

A - The Darkness of Death.

Q - Am I then to understand that Death the peculiar subject of this Degree.

A - It is indeed.

Q - When admitted into the Lodge how we you disposed of?

A - I was conducted between the Deacons to the Level of the Senior Warden and directed to advance as a Fellow Craft, first as an Entered Apprentice.

Q. - What were you then desired to do?

A - Kneel, and receive the benefit of Masonic prayer.

Q - Which I will thank you for.

A - Almighty and Eternal God, Architect and Ruler of the Universe, at whose creative fiat all things first were made, we, the frail creatures of Thy providence, humbly implore Thee to pour down on this convocation assembled in Thy Holy Name the continual dew of Thy blessing. Especially we beseech Thee to impart Thy grace to this Thy servant, who offers himself a candidate to partake with us the mysterious Secrets of a Master Mason. Endue him with such fortitude that in the hour of trial he fail not, but that passing safely under Thy protection, through the valley of the shadow of death, he may finally rise from the tomb of transgression, to shine as the stars for ever and ever.

So mote it be.

Q - After the recital of this prayer how were you disposed of?

A - I was conducted three times round the Lodge.

Q - What was required of you the first time?

A - To salute the Worshipful Master as a Mason, advance to the Junior Warden as such, showing the Sign and communicating the Token and Word.

Q - What was required of you the second time?

A - To salute the Worshipful Master and Junior Warden as a Fellow Craft, advance to the Senior Warden as such showing the Sign and communicating the Token and Word of that degree.

Q - What were the Brethren then called on to observe?

A - That I, who had been regularly initiated into Freemasonry, and passed to degree of a Fellow Craft was about to pass in view before them, to show that I was the candidate properly prepared to be raised to the sublime degree of a Master Mason.

Q - What was required of you the third time.

A - To salute the Worshipful Master and Junior Warden as a Fellow Craft, advance to the Senior Warden as such, show the Sign and communicating the Passing Grip and Passing Word leading from the Second to the Third Degree.

Q - How did the Senior Warden then proceed?

A - He presented me to the Right Worshipful Master as a candidate properly prepared to be raised the Third Degree.

Q - What did the Master then order?

A - The Senior Warden to direct the Deacons to instruct me to advance to the East by the proper steps.

Q - I will thank you to show the method of advancing from W. to E. in this degree.

A - Which is done.

Q - When placed. before the Master in the East how did he address you?

A - It is but fair to inform you that a most serious trial of your fortitude and fidelity, and a more Solemn Obligation await you. Are you prepared to meet them as you ought? To which I gave my assent.

Q. - What did the Master then desire you to.

A - Kneel on both knees, and place both hands on Volume of the Sacred Law.

Q - In that attitude, what were you to do?

A - Take the Solemn Obligation of a Master Mason.

Q - Which I will thank you for.

A - I, A. B., in the presence of the Most High, and of this worthy and worshipful Lodge of Master Masons, duly constituted, regularly assembled, and properly dedicated, of my own free will and accord do hereby and hereon most solemnly promise and swear, that I will always hele, conceal, and never reveal any or either of the secrets or mysteries of or belonging to the Degree of a Master Mason to anyone in the world, unless it be to him or them to whom the same may justly and lawfully belong; and not even to him or them, until after due trial, strict examination, or full conviction, that he or they are worthy of that confidence, or in the body of a Master Masons Lodge, duly opened on the Circle. I further solemnly pledge myself to adhere to the principles of the Square and Compasses, answer and obey all lawful signs, and summonses sent to me from a Master Masons Lodge, if within the length of my cable tow, and plead no excuse except sickness, or the pressing emergencies of my own public or private avocations. I further solemnly engage myself to maintain and uphold the Five Points of Fellowship. in act, as well as in word; that my Hand given to a Master Mason shall be a sure pledge of brotherhood; that my Feet shall travel through dangers and difficulties to unite with his in forming a column of mutual defence and support; that the Posture of my daily supplications shall remind me of his wants, and dispose my heart to succour his weakness and relieve his necessities, so far as may fairly be done without detriment to myself or connections; that my Breast shall be the sacred repository of his secrets when intrusted to my care- murder, treason, felony, and all other offences contrary to the laws of God, and the ordinances of the realm, being at all times most especially excepted, and, finally, that I will maintain a Master Masons honour, and carefully preserve it as my own. I Will not injure him myself, or knowingly suffer it to be done by others, if in my power to prevent it; but, on the contrary, will boldly repel the slanderer of his good name, and most strictly respect the chastity of those nearest and dearest to him, in the persons of his wife, his sister, and his child. All these points I solemnly swear to observe, without evasion, equivocation, or mental reservation of any kind, under no less a penalty, on the violation of any of them, than that of being, stomach being cut across, my entrials draw out and burnt before my living eyes and that my body be then burnt, that no trace or remembrance of so vile a wretch may longer be found among men, particularly Master Masons. So help me the Most High, and keep me steadfast in this my Solemn Obligation of a Master Mason.

Q - Having taken the Solemn Obligation of a Master Mason, what did the Master require of you?

A - As a pledge of my fidelity, and to render this binding as a Solemn Obligation for so long as I should live, to seal it with my lips on the Volume of the Sacred Law.

Q - How did he then address you?

A - Let me once more call your attention to the position of the Square and Compasses; when you were made an Entered Apprentice both points were hid, in the Second Degree one was disclosed: in this the whole is exhibited, implying that you are now at liberty to work with Both those Points in order to render the circle of your Masonic duties complete.

Q - How did the Master then proceed.

A - He friendly took me by the right hand and said, Rise, newly Obligated Master Mason.

Q - Repeat the exhortation.

A ‑ Having entered upon the Solemn Obligation of a Master Mason, you are now entitled to demand that last and greatest trial, by which alone you can be admitted to a participation of the secrets of this Degree. But it is first my duty to call your attention to a retrospect of those Degrees in Freemasonry through which you have already passed, that you may the better be enabled to distinguish and appreciate the connection of our whole system, and the relative dependency of its several parts. Your admission amongst Masons in a state of helpless indigence, was an emblematical representation of the entrance of all men on this their mortal existence; it inculcated the useful lessons of natural equality and mutual dependence; it instructed you, in the active principles of universal beneficence and clarity, to seek the solace of your own distress, by extending relief and consolation to your fellow-creatures in the hour of their affliction; above all, it taught you to bend with humility and resignation to the will of the Great Architect of the Universe; to dedicate your heart, thus purified from every baneful and malignant passion, fitted only for the reception of truth and wisdom, to His Glory and the welfare of your fellow‑ mortals.

Proceeding onwards, still guiding your progress by the principles of moral truth, you were led, in the Second Degree, to contemplate the intellectual faculty, and to trace it, from its development, through the paths of Heavenly science, even to the throne of God Himself. The secrets of nature and the principles of intellectual truth, were then unveiled to your view. To your mind, thus modelled by virtue and science, nature, however, presents one great and useful lesson more; she prepares you, by contemplation, for the closing hour of existence, and when, by means of that contemplation, she has conducted you through the intricate windings of this mortal life, she finally instructs you how to die.

Such, my Brother, are the peculiar objects of the Third Degree in Freemasonry; they invite you to reflect on this awful subject, and teach you to feel, that to the just and virtuous man death has no terrors equal to the stain of falsehood and dishonour. Of this great truth the annals of Masonry afford a glorious example, in the unshaken fidelity, and noble death, of our Master, Hiram Abif who was killed just before the completion of King Solomon's Temple, at the construction of which he was, as no doubt you are well aware, the principal Architect.

Q - As a Master Mason whence come you?

A - The East.

Q - Whither directing your course?

A - The West.

Q - What inducement have you to leave the East and go to the West?

A - To seek for that which was lost, which, by your instruction and our own industry, we hope to find.

Q - What is that which was lost?

A - The genuine secrets of a M. M.

Q - How came they lost?

A - By the untimely death of our Master Hiram Abif.

Q - I will thank you to inform me how our Master Hiram came by his death.

A - Fifteen Fellow Crafts, of that superior class appointed to preside over the rest, finding that the work was nearly completed, and that they were not in possession of the Secrets of the Third Degree, conspired to obtain them by any means, even to have recourse to violence; at the moment, however, of carrying their conspiracy into execution, twelve of the fifteen recanted, but three of a more determined and atrocious character than the rest, persisted in their impious design, in the prosecution of which they planted themselves respectively at the East North, and South entrances of the Temple, whither our Master had retired to pay his adoration to the MOST HIGH, as was his wonted custom at the hour of high twelve. Having finished his devotions, he attempted to return by the South entrance, where he was opposed by the first of those ruffians, who, for want of other weapon, had armed himself with a heavy Plumb Rule, and in a threatening manner demanded the secrets of a Master Mason, warning him that death would be the consequence of a refusal. Our Master, true to his Obligation, answered that those secrets were known to but three in the world, and that, without the consent and co- operation of the other two he neither could, nor would, divulge them, but intimated that he had no doubt patience and industry would in due time entitle the worthy Mason to a participation of them, but that, for his own part, he would rather suffer death than betray the sacred trust reposed in him. This answer not proving satisfactory, the ruffian aimed a violent blow at the head of our Master, but being startled at the firmness of his demeanour, it missed his forehead, and only glanced on his right temple but with such force as to cause him to reel and sink on his left knee. Recovering from the shock, he made for the North entrance were he was accosted by the second of those ruffians, to whom he gave a similar answer with undiminished firmness, when the ruffian, who was armed with a Level, struck him a violent blow on the Left temple, which brought him to the ground on his right knee. Finding his retreat cut off at both those points, he staggered faint and bleeding to the East entrance, where the third ruffian was posted who received a similar answer to his insolent demand (for even at this trying moment our Master remained firm and unshaken), when the villain, who was armed with a heavy maul, stuck him a violent blow on the forehead, which laid him lifeless at his feet.

Q - When you lying extended on the ground in this degree in Freemasonry, how did the Master address the Lodge?

A - The Brethren will take notice, that in the recent ceremony, as well as in his present situation, our Brother has been made to represent one of the brightest characters recorded in the annals of Masonry, namely, Hiram Abif, who lost his life in consequence of his unshaken fidelity to the sacred trust reposed in him; and I hope this will make a lasting impression on his and your minds, should you ever be placed in a similar state of trial.

Q - What did he then order?

A - The Junior Warden to endeavour to raise me by the Entered Apprentice's grip, which proved a slip.

Q - What did he next order?

A - The Senior Warden to try the Fellow Craft's, which proved a slip likewise.

Q - How did the Master then address his principal officers?

A - Bro. Wardens, having both failed in your attempts, there remains a third method, by taking a more firm hold of the sinews of the hand and raising him on the Five Point's of Fellowship, which with your assistance I will make trial of.

Q - Were you raised, and on what?

A - I was, on the Five Points of Fellowship.

Q - What enabled you to be raised to the sublime Degree of a Master Mason?

A - The help of God, the united aid of the Square and Compasses and my own industry.

Q - From what and to what were you Raised?

A - From the Square to the Compasses or from a superficial fiat to a lively perpendicular Q - How did the Master then address you?

A - It is thus all Master Masons are raised from a figurative death to a reunion with the former companions of their toils.

Q - Repeat the charge.

A - Let me now beg you to observe, that the light of a Master Mason is darkness visible, serving only to express that gloom which rests on the prospect of futurity; it is that mysterious veil which the eye of human reason cannot penetrate, unless assisted by that light which is from above; yet, even by this glimmering ray, you may perceive that you stand on the very brink of the grave into which you have just figuratively descended, and which, when this transitory life shall have passed away, will again receive you into its cold bosom. Let the emblems of mortality which lie before you, lead you to contemplate on your inevitable destiny, and guide your reflections to that most interesting of all human studies, the knowledge of yourself. Be careful to perform your allotted task while it is yet day; continue to listen to the voice of nature, which bears witness, that even in this perishable frame, resides a vital and immortal principle, which inspires a holy confidence that the Lord of life will enable us to trample the king of terrors beneath our feet, and lift our eyes to that bright morning star, whose rising, brings peace and salvation to the faithful and obedient of the human race.

Q - How did the Master then address you?

A - I cannot better reward the attention you have paid to this exhortation and Charge, than by intrusting you with the secrets of the degree; you will therefore advance to me as a Fellow Craft first as an Entered Apprentice.

Q - What did he next direct you to do?

A - Take another step towards him with my left foot bringing the right heel into its hollow as before; that, the Worshipful Master informed me, is the third regular step in Freemasonry, and it is in this position that the secrets of the degree are communicated.

Q - Of what do those secrets consist?

A - Signs, a Token, and Word.

Q - Having been Obligated and intrusted, what permission did
you then receive?

A - To retire, in order to restore myself to my personal comforts,
and the Worshipful Master informed me that on my return
to the Lodge the signs token and word would be further explained.

CHARGE

*May the fragrance of Virtue like the sprig of Acacia bloom over the
grave of every deceased Bro.*

SECTION TWO

Q - On your return to the Lodge were you invested?

A - I was, with the distinguishing badge of a Master Mason, which the Senior Warden informed me was to mark the further progress I had made in the science.

Q - Repeat the address you then received from the Master.

A - I must state, that the badge with which you have now been invested, not only points out your rank as a Master Mason but is meant to remind you of those great duties you have just solemnly engaged yourself to observe; and whilst it marks your own superiority, it calls on you to afford assistance and instruction to the Brethren in the inferior Degrees.

Q - We left off at that part of our traditional history which mentions the death of our Master, Hiram Abiff; what effect had this melancholy event on the Craft?

A - A loss so important as that of the principal architect, could not fail of being generally and severely felt; the want of those plans and designs, which had hitherto been regularly supplied to the different classes of workmen, was the first indication that some heavy calamity had befallen our Master; the Menatschin or Prefects, or, more familiarly speaking, the Overseers, deputed some of the most eminent of their number to acquaint King Solomon with the utter confusion into which the absence of Hiram had plunged them, and to express their apprehension that to some fatal catastrophe must be attributed his sudden and mysterious disappearance.

Q - What did King Solomon then order?

A - A general muster of the workmen throughout the different departments, when three of the same class of overseers were not to be found. On the same day, the twelve craftsmen who had originally joined in the conspiracy came before the King, and made a voluntary confession of all they knew, down to the time of withdrawing themselves from the number of the conspirators.

Q - How did he then proceed?

A - His fears being naturally increased for the safety of his chief artist, he selected fifteen trusty Fellow Crafts and ordered them to make diligent search after the person of our Master to ascertain if he were yet alive, or had suffered .death in the attempt to extort from him the secrets of his exalted degree.

Q - What measures did those Craftsmen take?

A - A stated day having been appointed for their return to Jerusalem, they formed themselves into three Fellow Craft's, Lodges, and departed from the three entrances of the Temple. Many days were spent in fruitless search; indeed, one class returned without having made any discovery of importance.

Q - Were a second class more fortunate?

A - They were, for on the evening of a certain day, after having suffered the greatest privations and personal fatigues, one of the Brethren who had rested himself in a reclining posture, to assist his rising, caught hold of a shrub that grew near, which, to his surprise, came easily out of the ground; on a closer examination, he found that the earth had been recently disturbed; he therefore hailed his companions, and with their united endeavours reopened the grave and there found the body of our Master very indecently interred. They covered it again with all respect and reverence, and to distinguish the spot, stuck a sprig of acacia at the head of the grave; they then hastened to Jerusalem to impart the afflicting intelligence to King Solomon.

Q - How did King Solomon proceed on hearing this melancholy report?

A - When the first emotions of his grief had subsided, he ordered them to return, and raise our Master to such a sepulture as became his rank and exalted talents; at the same time informing them that by his untimely death the secrets of a Master Mason were lost; he therefore charged them to be particularly careful in observing whatever casual Signs, Tokens, or Words might occur, whilst paying this last sad tribute of respect to departed merit.

Q - Did they perform their task?

A - They did, with the utmost fidelity, and on reopening the grave one of the Brethren looking round, observed some of his companions in this position, smitten with horror at the dreadful and afflicting sight; while others, viewing the grief which was still visible on his features, their own in sympathy with his sufferings. Three of the Brethren then descended the grave and endeavoured to raise him by the Entered Apprentice's Grip, which proved a slip; they then tried the Fellow Craft's which proved a slip likewise; having both failed in their attempts, a zealous and expert Brother took a more firm hold of the sinews of the wrist, and with their assistance raised him on the Five Points of Fellowship, whilst others, more animated, exclaimed words having a nearly similar import; one signifying the death of the builder, the other the builder is smitten.

Q - What did King Solomon then order?

A - That those casual Signs, and that Token and Word, should designate all Master Masons throughout the universe, until time or circumstances should restore the genuine.

Q - What became of the third class?

A - They had pursued their researches in the direction of Joppa, and were meditating their return to Jerusalem, when, accidentally passing the mouth of a cavern, they heard sounds of deep lamentation and regret. On entering the cave to ascertain the cause, they found three men answering the description of those missing, who, on being charged with the murder, and finding all chance of escape cut off, made a full confession of their guilt. They were then bound and led to Jerusalem, when King Solomon sentenced them to that death the heinousness of their crime so amply merited.

Q - Where was our Master ordered to be reinterred?

A - As near to the Sanctum Sanctorum as the Israelitish law would permit; there in a grave, from the centre three feet East and three feet West, three feet between North and South, and five feet or more perpendicular.

Q - Why not in the Sanctum Sanctorum?

A - Because nothing common or unclean was allowed to enter there; not even the High Priest but once a year; nor then until after many washings and purifications against the great day of expiation for sins, for by the Israelitish law all flesh was deemed unclean.

Q - Who were ordered to attend the funeral?

A - The same fifteen trusty Fellow Crafts clothed in white Aprons and Gloves, as emblems of their innocence.

CHARGE

To him who did the Temple rear,
Who lived and died within the same,
and now lies buried none know where,
But we who Master Masons are.

SECTION THREE

Q - Name the Ornaments of a Master Mason's Lodge.

A - The Porch, Dormer, and Square pavement.

Q - Their uses?

A - The Porch was the entrance to the Sanctum Sanctorum; the Dormer the window that gave light to the same; and the Square pavement for the High Priest to walk on.

Q - The High Priest's office?

A - To burn incense to the honour and glory of the Most High, and to pray fervently that the Almighty, of His unbounded wisdom and goodness, would be pleased to bestow peace and tranquillity on the Israelitish nation during the ensuring year.

Q - Name, the Pass Word leading from the Second to the Third Degree.

A. (This is done)

Q - Who was Tubel-Cain?

A - The first artificer in metals.

Q - The import of his name?

A - Worldly possessions.

Q - Name the Five Points of Fellowship.

A - Hand to Hand, Foot to Foot, Knee to Knee Breast to Breast, and Hand over Back.

Q - Explain them briefly.

A - Hand to hand, I greet you as a Brother. Foot to foot, I will support you in all your laudable undertakings. Knee to knee, the posture of my daily supplications shall remind me of your wants. Breast to breast, your lawful secrets, when intrusted to me as such, I will keep as my own. A Hand over back, I will support your character in your absence as in your presence.

Q - Explain them at length.

A - Hand to hand, when the necessities of a Brother call for aid, we should not be backward in stretching forth the hand, to render the assistance which might save him from sinking, knowing him to be worthy, and that no being detrimental to ourselves or connections Foot to foot, indolence should not cause our feet to halt, nor wrath turn our steps aside, but forgetting every selfish consideration, and remembering that man was not born for his own enjoyment alone, but for the assistance of his generation, we should be swift of foot to help, aid, and execute benevolence to a fellow-creature, particularly a Brother Mason. Knee to knee when we offer up our ejaculations to the Most High a Brother's welfare we should remember as our own, for as the voice of babes and sucklings are heard at the throne of grace, so most assuredly will the breathings of a fervent and contrite heart reach the dominions of bliss; our prayers being reciprocally required for each other' welfare. Breast to breast, a Brother's. lawful secrets, when intrusted to us as such, we should keep as our own; for to betray the trust which one Brother reposes in another, might be to do him the greatest injury he could possibly receive in this life; nay, it would be like the villany of the assassin who, lurking in darkness, stabs his adversary to the heart when unarmed and in all probability least suspicious of danger. Hand over back, a Brother's character we should support absent or present; we should not revile him ourselves, or knowingly suffer it to be done by others. Thus, Brethren by the Five Points of Fellowship ought we to be united in one sincere bond of fraternal affection, which will sufficiently serve to distinguish us from those who are strangers to our Masonic Order and may demonstrate to the world, in general, that the word Brother among Masons is something more than a name.

Q - Name the working tools of a Master Mason.

A - The Scurret, Pencil, and Compasses.

Q - Their uses?

A - The Scurret is an implement which acts on a centre pin, whence a line is drawn to mark out ground for the foundation of the intended structure; with the Pencil the skilful artist delineates the building in a draft or plan, for the instruction and guidance of the workmen; the Compasses enable him with accuracy and precision to ascertain and determine the limits and proportions of its several parts.

Q - But as we are not all Operative Masons, but rather Free and Accepted, or Speculative, how do we apply these tools to our morals?

A - In this sense, the Scurret points out that straight and undeviating line of conduct laid down for our pursuit in the Volume of the Sacred Law; the Pencil teaches us that our words and actions are observed and recorded by the Almighty Architect, to whom we must give an account of our conduct through life; the Compasses remind us of His unerring and impartial justice, Who, having defined for our instruction the limits of good and evil, will reward or punish, as we have obeyed or disregarded His divine commands. Thus, the working tools of a Master Mason teach us to bear in mind, and act according to, the laws of our Divine Creator, that when we shall be summoned from this sublunary abode, we may ascend to the Grand Lodge above, where the world's great Architect lives and reigns forever.

CHARGE

To him who most things understood,
To him who found the stones and wood,
And him who nobly spilt his blood.
In the doing of his duty.
Blessed be the age, and blessed each morn,
On which those three great men were born,
Who Israel's Temple did adorn
With Wisdom, Strength, and Beauty.

MASONICA

Publishers of the Ancient Craft